3 DECADES COLD

C. McMULLIN
MARIA VIOLA JEFFERSON

Milwaukee Wisconsin USA

3 Decades Cold
Copyright © 2024 Chris McMullin and Maria Viola Jefferson

Published by:
Genius Book Publishing
PO Box 250380
Milwaukee Wisconsin 53225 USA
GeniusBookPublishing.com

ISBN: 978-1-958727-35-5

240517 HQ

Contents

This book is dedicated to the victims and their families.

Acknowledgments

I would like to acknowledge and thank those who have had the greatest impact on the success of this book.

Mike Mosniak, Jennifer Schorn, and Jess Bryant. Without the three of them the Rowan case would not have been solved.

Honorable mention goes out to the support given to us by David Nieves, John Monaghan, Tim Carroll, and Jennifer Spears.

Frank Friel, who believed in me and gave me my shot at my career.

Yolanda McClary, who was instrumental in identifying Lisa Todd.

Jennifer Moore, who was equally instrumental in identifying Merrybeth Hodgkinson.

Fred Harran, for giving me the things I needed to work these cases.

Heather Hines, Caitlin, Mom and Dad.

PROLOGUE

Some say I have a knack for solving cold cases. I don't know if I would go as far as to say that, but I can't stand unsolved cases and think of everything I can do to solve them. It's not talent; it's pure stubbornness. I'd rather go down in flames trying than not trying. I was born and raised in Philadelphia, and just like my city, I don't quit. Philly is known as the city of underdogs. An underdog is someone thought to have little chance of success or winning. I took on several unsolved cases that I was told I'd never solve or had little chance of solving. I like being the underdog.

Three decades was the average age of every cold case I reopened. Some we solved, some we partially solved, others are still a mystery. These are some examples of those cases along with some current ones. I had a lot of good times and bad during this stretch of my life and career. This book will provide a look into those experiences.

I never knew Barbara Rowan; we never met in life. Nonetheless, we shared some of the same friends in Trevose, Pennsylvania. I learned about her death in 1984 long before I could do something about it. When I was a fourteen-year-old kid, my bus passed by her house every day on the way to summer camp. Her murderer escaped his fate for thirty-three years. Little did I know the future would connect me to Barbara once again in my adult life. Her unsolved murder was my first cold case investigation. I felt like an idiot crying to Paula Zahn on national television. But it was time to let it all out. After all, Barbara Rowan is the reason I began working on cold cases.

Although I never knew Lisa Todd, I spent nineteen years watching over her as the "Publicker Jane Doe," aka "Bucks County Jane Doe." She was missing for thirty-six years, and thirty-three of them went by before police finally learned her identity. In 1988, her skeletal remains were found at the bottom of an old pump house at the abandoned Publicker Distillery on State Road in Bensalem, Pennsylvania. Investigators discovered she was pregnant at the time of death after finding a set of fetal bones within her remains. The cause and manner of death were listed as undetermined. The police released a detailed forensic sculpture of her face created by renowned forensic artist Frank Bender to the public through mass media. But year after year, she sadly remained unidentified.

In 1984, twenty-two-year-old Jeanette Tambe left her troubled home life in Bensalem, Pennsylvania, never to be seen again. Two years later, in 1986, her unidentified body was discovered in a wooded lot behind a house under construction in Buena Vista Township, New Jersey. She, too, had become a Jane Doe statistic and would remain unidentified as "Buena Vista Jane Doe" for another 26 years.

Jeanette's death was very violent. Her hands and feet were shackled with pipe hangers. Multiple superficial stab wounds to her abdomen indicated that she had been tortured before dying. Her killer then poured sulfuric acid on her face, chest, and throat.

I initially thought there was a good chance that Jeanette could be my Publicker Jane Doe until the lab matched the DNA from Jeanette's brother to Buena Vista Jane Doe. This ultimately led to us identifying her as Jeanette Tambe. This revelation was significant because it solved the long-term missing person case of Jeanette Tambe and identified Buena Vista Jane Doe. But it still left us with the million-dollar question: Who was Publicker Jane Doe?

In 2002, I reopened the case of fourteen-year-old Tracy Byrd, who went missing in March 1983. She was last seen by Paul Greenwald, her mom's boyfriend, when he dropped her off at Bensalem High School. Records show that she never attended school that day and was marked absent. At one time, I thought Tracy could be my Publicker Jane Doe due to the location of the remains, the time frame, and the physical commonalities they shared. But DNA samples from Tracy's family were not a match for Publicker Jane Doe. Sadly, Tracy Byrd is still missing, but I have one more idea for how to find her.

My career as a detective has been about more than just solving cold cases. I've seen and heard some horrible things while working in the Bensalem Police Department's Special Victims Unit (SVU) over the years. On a positive note, I've had the satisfaction of taking some awful people off the streets—murderers, sexual predators, and violent criminals. You get my point. But doing this kind of work comes with a price—my job isn't ever over at the end of the day. I've always had a hard time "turning it off," and at times, it can be mentally crippling. It has undoubtedly affected my personal life. Yet, I've had some highlights throughout my career, and retirement is now close. But it's been a hell of a ride, and the cases discussed in this book are only a fraction of my experiences on the job.

Here's another: James Lawrence was one of Christian Rojas' best friends. Christian referred to James' mother, Janet, as his "American mom." James had been out of town and arranged for Christian to pick him up from the Philadelphia International Airport. More than an hour went by while James waited. Christian was usually a reliable and responsible friend, and this was not characteristic of him. When James couldn't contact Christian, he called another friend to pick him up and take him to Christian's apartment. James knocked at the front door of Christian's ground-floor apartment, but there was no answer. James found the back sliding door unlocked and walked in. Once inside, he called out for Christian and received no response. He walked around the apartment to investigate and discovered a horrific scene.

My job also requires the ugly task of investigating sex crimes. One Saturday morning in July 2010, a woman came into headquarters to file a formal complaint about her ex-boyfriend, Walter Meyerle, who had sexually abused her daughter. She stated she had initially reported the incident in 1999. However, since her daughter was only five years old then, she did not want her to endure the traumatic process of being interviewed and going to court, so the police did not conduct an investigation, upon her request. Now that her daughter was older (sixteen), the abuse was beginning to negatively affect her—traumatic memories had begun to resurface, and she desperately needed counseling. As it turned out, she was not his only victim.

Each of these criminal cases has affected my life in one form or another. But at the end of the day, it's not about me—it's about the victims and the impact on their families. My job is to make a positive difference.

CHAPTER 1
The Early Years

I graduated from the Philadelphia Police Academy in class 294 on March 25, 1991. My grandmother—"Nan," as I liked to call her—threw a party for me at her home in the Mayfair section of Philadelphia. There was a big cake with my badge number, 4487. As I observed family, friends, and loved ones celebrating this turning point, I couldn't help but reflect on what led me there.

Lexington Park, Philadelphia, is where I grew up with my parents. But some of my fondest memories are from Nan's summer home. In the summer of 1977, I was a skinny seven-year-old kid. The Wildwoods were, and still are, known as one of the most popular places along the South Jersey shoreline. Nan's place was right next door to the North Wildwood Police Department, and from the time I was about four years old, I would watch the police officers from our front porch. I loved spending summers at my Nan's because it was much more fun than the neighborhood in Philly. You can always enjoy five miles of beach and boardwalk rides, arcades, and shops.

On a typical hot and humid summer day at the Jersey Shore, I was riding my bike in front of Nan's house when I fell. Two officers saw me and got out of their patrol car to help. They recognized me as the kid who lived in the house next to the police station. From that day forward, the same two officers always waved at me when they passed by. They were genuinely good guys. I remember seeing their cruiser up close with the door open, and hearing the crackle of the police radio amazed me. Day in and day out, summer after summer, I watched the officers of the North Wildwood Police Department protect and serve their community.

Fast forward ten years later to May 7, 1987, the day of my junior prom. My beautiful daughter, Caitlin, was born. Needless to say, I didn't go to the dance. I was seventeen and in eleventh grade, so I had another year until graduation. I attended Catholic school, and some priests broke my balls over being a teen parent. They had to play the role, after all. They felt they were doing the right thing. We named our daughter after Caitlin Davies from the popular 1980s television series *Miami Vice*. Actress and singer Sheena Easton played this role of Sonny Crockett's wife on the show.

Caitlin's mom, "Marie," and I met through mutual friends in the spring of 1986. I've decided to use a false name in this bio for her and her family's privacy. I was sixteen years old. My parents were divorced, and I lived with my father in Northeast Philadelphia. For the record, I didn't choose my father over my mom; I didn't want to leave home. My father refused to leave our house in Northeast Philly for years. Because of this, my mother had no choice but to move out.

One summer night, when I was eleven or twelve years old, my parents and I were driving to the shore in my dad's '76 Cadillac Coupe Deville. I fell asleep in the backseat because it was late and dark. When I woke up, my parents were arguing but trying to keep it down so they wouldn't wake me. They could have been more successful. I didn't sit up; I just lay there pretending to be asleep in the back seat. I was afraid if I sat up, I'd get yelled at. I could feel the tenacity and anger in my mom's voice as they went back and forth at each other; she was practically spitting venom at him. My father was driving and didn't say as much, but he clearly was disgusted as it radiated through his voice when he responded. Have you ever heard two people try to argue quietly? It doesn't work. That was the first time I heard the song "Hearts" by Marty Balin, and now, any time I hear it, it reminds me of that night in my dad's car—it has stuck with me forever.

When Marie and I got together, she lived in the nearby Mayfair section, and her parents had split up by then too. It was my first real relationship. When she got pregnant, our lives changed forever. I remember she had a pregnancy test done at the local free clinic, and, as it turned out, she was nineteen weeks along. It was clear she had been holding out on me. I panicked initially; I knew I had to tell my parents.

Thanksgiving Eve 1986, we told my father about the pregnancy—he was the first to know. He was disgusted with us and called my mom first, then Marie's parents. Everyone gathered at my father's house, and our mothers were very emotional; they both cried and fell apart. Our fathers were even-tempered yet heavy-handed. They laid down the law and told us we would put the baby up for adoption. They didn't ask or suggest; they just told us. I disagreed with the "plans," but we were too afraid to speak up against them. We were kids; we couldn't provide for a baby and hadn't even graduated high school. I only agreed to the adoption to get them off our backs. I told Marie to play along with them, and she did. Workers from the adoption agency visited us every week, but we never met the people who planned to adopt Caitlin.

Nan was the only person I could talk to in our family. She knew I didn't want to give up the baby, but I was scared. I didn't know how we would take care of a baby. Where would we live? How could I pay the bills? I'll never forget the day my Nan turned to look at me and said sternly, "We will pay the bills. Don't let that be a reason to give up the baby." I had no intention of going through with the adoption, but I dreaded facing our fathers over it.

Each of our mothers showed up at the hospital the day Marie went into labor, but our fathers were absent. We were at the hospital all night as she gave birth to a beautiful baby girl, Caitlin. Our decision to keep the baby caused a huge wedge between my dad and me. Eventually, I moved out to live with Nan in the neighboring Mayfair section of Philadelphia. Caitlin stayed with her mother, who lived just two blocks from Nan's house.

I *attended* Father Judge Catholic High School in Northeast Philadelphia. I emphasize "attended" because I didn't learn a thing there, except how to talk my way out of detention, aka JUG—"Justice Under God." I was a terrible student and went to summer school two out of my four years there. The nuns at St. Hubert's High School wouldn't let Marie attend school once she started showing. But after Caitlin was born, she returned to school and graduated on time.

Father Kilty, academic dean, and my English teacher was very good to me while the other priests looked down on me. He was the kind of guy who would sit me down with a cigarette in his mouth and have casual heart-to-heart talks. Occasionally I'd bum a smoke off him too.

He also baptized Caitlin. That day played out interestingly with my dysfunctional family. Imagine: My mother and Nan weren't talking to my father. My father and his girlfriend sat on the other side of the church. On top of that, Marie's parents were separated and didn't want to sit next to one another. It was so awkward that at one point, Father Kilty announced, "Let's remember Caitlin is here for a purpose."

Twenty years later, Caitlin was attending nursing school while Nan was dying. Caitlin jumped in and took fantastic care of Nan. My mother and I would never have been able to go through it without Caitlin. Father Kilty's declaration ultimately rang true.

Father Kilty was different from the other priests—he never lectured or shamed me in any way. He didn't speak down to me as an adolescent. Instead, he was honest with me. I always knew where I stood with him and never left the room confused. When I learned I would be a father, I sat down with him and said, "I fucked up." And he replied, "Yeah, you did fuck up. But you fucked up once, and you could've fucked up twice by getting an abortion, and you didn't." I felt like a man in his presence, not an irresponsible teenager who got a girl pregnant.

Father Kilty would tell me stories about my great-uncle, who was in the priesthood. Monsignor Joseph McMullin died when I was four years old. I have no memory of him, but he did baptize me. He taught at Saint Charles Borromeo Seminary in Wynnewood, Pennsylvania, just outside Philadelphia.

Monsignor McMullin, or "Holy Joe The Hammer," as they called him, spoke thirteen languages. Father Kilty was one of his students at the seminary before he was ordained. I understood the nickname "Holy Joe," but I asked Father Kilty why they called him "The Hammer." Kilty laughed and said my great-uncle enjoyed telling jokes and was known for knocking a firm elbow into the recipient's arm and saying, "Did you get it, did you get it, did you get it?" Hence, "The Hammer." Years later, Father Kilty transferred to a different school, and we eventually lost touch. However, he left a lifelong impression on me, and I will always be grateful for the time we spent getting to know each other.

When I graduated high school, I knew I wanted to become a police officer. All those years sitting on the front porch in North Wildwood lit a fire in me, and I no longer wanted to watch the cops; I wanted to be one. My father and I were now on good terms, although he didn't like where I was in life. Nan still had her summer house in North Wildwood and her primary home in Mayfair. I was able to live with her while going to college part-time. I worked at the Friendship Pharmacy and Spitzer's Mobil Station. I also mowed lawns to help support Caitlin financially.

In the summer of 1989, I interviewed for a seasonal dispatcher position at the North Wildwood Police Department (NWPD) with Captain Gary Sloan. He was in his forties and stood about six feet tall. He had a calm demeanor about him. During the interview, he questioned why I wanted to be in law enforcement, and I replied, "I want to help people." Captain Sloan then asked, "Do you have any relatives in law enforcement?" I answered, "None that I've ever met." Nan had told me about relatives I never knew in New York City who were on the job. She once mentioned that I had a great uncle, Mickey Finnigan, who was in the NYPD and walked a beat in Harlem.

"Are you ready to work for the North Wildwood Police Department?" asked Captain Sloan. I smiled and said, "Yes, I am." Captain Sloan emphasized the importance of getting to know the town's citizens and, in his words, stated, "Do little things, too… like helping little kids up when they fall off their bikes." He smiled, then told me I had the job. If you haven't caught on yet, he was one of the police officers who helped me when I fell off my bike in 1977. He remembered me, and I began working as a seasonal dispatcher for the NWPD.

The second officer who helped me when I fell off my bike that day was Anthony J. Sittineri. He had since become the chief of police. He was an old-school street cop described by other cops as "a cop's cop." One evening, I was working in dispatch and received a call from Chief Sittineri's youngest daughter, Sharon. Her older sister had just given birth to her first child. Sharon asked if I could announce over the police radio that Chief Sittineri had just become a grandfather.

I was the new guy and hadn't been working there long. I didn't know if I should make a broadcast over the police radio about the chief's family, but on the flip side, I didn't want to refuse a request from the chief's daughter, so I told her I would do it. I figured he would either be pleased or fire me. I keyed up the mic and said, "Two to 200." (NWPD was District Two, and the chief's call sign was 200). He responded, "200." As you may have guessed from the name Sittineri, he was Italian and had that old-school Italian way about him that I loved. I replied, "Your youngest daughter called; congratulations, you're a grandfather." He didn't acknowledge the announcement immediately, and I got scared, thinking he would fire me or have me whacked out. After a few seconds, he finally replied with a typical "Ten-four."

A few minutes later, Lieutenant Jake Stevenson walked into HQ, and I again thought I was toast. Instead, he approached the dispatch window and commented, "That's great!" As it turned out, he, and more importantly, the chief, was happy I had broadcast the news.

One year later, I began working as a part-time police officer for the NWPD. May 14, 1990 marked the day I started training at the Cape May County Police Academy as a North Wildwood Class II Officer cadet. Being a cadet was a whole new ball game compared to working as a dispatcher. I had no idea what I was in for. It was grueling, military-style training, six days a week for seven weeks. The course was not as long as full-time police officer academies, but it was strict with a military atmosphere.

We were required to have crew cuts, be clean-shaven, and wear khaki uniforms. We marched and got yelled at by the drill instructors constantly. I laugh about it now but was not too fond of it back then; actually, I hated it.

Day one at the academy started with seventy-two cadets from all over the tri-state area assembled as the 5th Special Class. Only forty-two of us made it to graduation day. Thirty cadets washed out for a variety of reasons. Some couldn't handle the physical training. I recall one guy who failed the drug screening. Some couldn't qualify with their firearms. The rest quit.

The physical training was demanding. The instructors pushed and ran us until we fell or puked, sometimes both. I was never a star athlete but managed to hang in there. I refused to give up and forced myself to suck it up. If you've ever watched the movie *An Officer and a Gentleman*, I adopted the dialogue and mentality portrayed by Richard

Gere's character, Zack Mayo: "You can kick me out, but I ain't quitting!"

During our workouts, we wore white T-shirts with our last names in black lettering on the front and dark blue sweatpants with our last names in white lettering on our asses. That way, no matter which direction we were facing, the drill instructors could yell at us by name, and they did so constantly.

In the gym, we had a formation to abide by, and we each had a designated spot to stand in. At any given time, a drill instructor would yell out your name, and you would have to respond loud and clear, "Yes, sir!" If he ordered you to "take the stand," then you would run like hell to the front of the class. Then he would say, "McMullin, lead the class in squat thrust exercises." The proper way to do this would be to address the class loudly and say, "Class, squat thrust exercises, starting positions... move! Ready... by the numbers... exercise! One-two-three, ONE! One-two-three, TWO! One-two-three, THREE!" and so on. If whoever was on the stand did not give the exercise order using those exact words, the instructors would punish the rest of the class with additional exercises, which sucked! I was in excellent physical condition by the time we graduated—I wish I were in such good shape now.

When the time came to go to the shooting range, I was nervous. I had never fired a handgun in my life. My father had taught me how to shoot shotguns and rifles before, but handguns were a new experience. By the grace of God, I shot well enough to score a passing grade.

Later that September, I was hired by the Philadelphia Police Department. One good thing about the intensity of the Cape May County Academy was that it prepared me for the Philadelphia Police Academy. Since my new job would be in a different state, I had to attend their academy before I could work there.

I began my training at the Philadelphia Police Academy in October. Although Philly was hard, it was not nearly as grueling as Cape May. The stressful environment they created at the Cape May County Academy was so much harsher. Drill instructors constantly scrutinized and yelled at the cadets to try to break us down. They were shaping us into rugged individuals, mentally and physically.

The day after I graduated from the Philadelphia Police Academy, I bought a house in the Holmesburg neighborhood of Philadelphia. I moved Caitlin and her mother in with me. Marie wanted to get married even though we weren't getting along. Our parents knew we didn't belong together, but, despite their opposition, we got married at a courthouse. It was for all the wrong reasons—mainly so Marie could have medical coverage under my health benefits. She had recently sustained a life-threatening asthma attack that had put her in the hospital for ten days, and I wanted to provide her with the best medical care possible.

The marriage lasted less than a year. Marie later met another guy, who she married and settled down with. They're still together, and I'm happy for them.

During the graduation party Nan threw for me, I found my mother on the second floor of Nan's house, crying. She was afraid something terrible would happen to me as a police officer. At first, I didn't understand. But I soon realized that my two summers as a seasonal cop in North Wildwood didn't concern her nearly as much as me working in Philadelphia. She grew up in the Bronx, New York, and my dad is from Philadelphia. When they were engaged, my dad got accepted into the NYPD and made plans to move to NYC. But my mother didn't want him to be a cop, so they moved to Philly instead, and my dad kept his job as a machinist at the Philadelphia Navy Yard.

So there I was, doing exactly what she had kept my father from doing, which devastated her. From that point on, I understood why it bothered her so much. I could only assure her I would be safe, and I've kept that promise so far.

CHAPTER 2
Bensalem

At the young age of twenty-two, I had been a Philadelphia Police officer for close to two years. I decided to leave Philadelphia, and on August 20, 1992, District Justice Leonard Brown swore me in as a Bensalem Police officer. I arrived at the Bensalem Police Department at 9 a.m. sharp. The director of public safety, Frank Friel, greeted me. Frank had been running the Bensalem PD since 1989. He was a retired Philadelphia Police captain and had made a name for himself in the Organized Crime Task Force. During his seasoned career in Philadelphia, he led the investigation that helped cripple the Philadelphia Mob and put notorious mob boss Nicodemus "Little Nicky" Scarfo in prison.

Nicky Scarfo stood only five feet, five inches tall, and weighed 135 pounds. Still, his terrifying acts of violent behavior and aggressiveness led to Scarfo becoming one of the nation's most feared organized crime figures. Eventually, he was imprisoned after being found guilty on nine counts of murder charges in addition to racketeering, extortion, gambling, and numerous other crimes, according to a 2017 article from the *New York Times*. In 2017, Scarfo passed away in prison at the age of eighty-seven.

A controversial television interview on the Philadelphia-based talk show *AM Philadelphia* aired on July 3, 1995, featuring Frank and renowned Philadelphia disc jockeys Jerry Blavat and Hy Lit.

Blavat was legendary for his significant influence in promoting pop music in the 1960s. His independent radio show served as a platform to introduce many acts to a broad audience, including the Isley Brothers and Frankie Valli and the Four Seasons. He also produced and hosted a weekly television show called *The Discophonic Scene*.

Lit, another Philadelphia disc jockey and radio personality from the 1950s and '60s, is most known for his *Hall of Fame* show, which dominated AM radio in Philadelphia. He later hosted the nationally syndicated *Hy Lit Show* in the late 1960s. Musical acts such as The Fifth Dimension, The Monkees, The Four Tops, and Marvin Gaye were among the weekly guests on the show. Lit was known to be Blavat's most significant competition back then.

Frank was still my boss during the interview and did media consultation work on the mafia. The broadcast brought the three men together to discuss Blavat's known mob ties and the circulating rumors that he had hired a hit man to take Lit out as the competition. Allegedly,

Blavat had asked Scarfo to have Lit killed to eliminate the competition, claiming Lit was taking business away from him.

Lit learned of the alleged hit through an unnamed telephone informant. But there was no concrete evidence of a hired hit, and no arrests had ever been made. Host Wally Kennedy asked Frank about his expert knowledge concerning Blavat and his suspected mob ties. He confirmed the relationship between Blavat and the mob, particularly Scarfo, throughout past police investigations. Blavat did not refute his association with Scarfo but repeatedly denied any wrongdoing. Ultimately, Lit and Blavat put the incident behind them and parted as friends.

Years later, Blavat was a guest at the local Screen Actors Guild meeting held at the Philadelphia SugarHouse Casino in September 2012. I had the pleasure of meeting him that night, and we spoke to each other warmly. When I mentioned knowing Frank, he smiled and said good things about him. It seemed as though there were no hard feelings. Blavat was a gentleman, and I enjoyed meeting "The Geator with the Heater," aka "The Boss with the Hot Sauce." These are monikers that Blavat used when performing as part of his show.

Frank successfully wrote and published a book titled *Breaking the Mob*, which tells the story of his investigations into the Philly Mob. Of course, I felt compelled to purchase the book and read it. One day in 1993, I asked Frank if he would autograph my book, and he smiled, said, "Come on in here, young man," and invited me into his office. He would always start the conversation with "young man" and finish with "my boy." Frank was the type of man who always appeared professional and well-dressed in a three-piece suit.

I noticed a large bust on his credenza when I entered his office. It was a sculpture of a young woman, and I asked who she was. He answered, "That, my dear boy, is the question." He explained that the sculpture was cast from the skull of a Jane Doe discovered in January 1988.

Her skeletal remains were found in an underground pumphouse of the defunct Publicker Distillery on State Road near the Delaware River. Frank informed me that renowned forensic artist Frank Bender of the Vidocq Society had created the sculpture.

The Vidocq Society is an organization of professionals from law enforcement, forensics, doctors, etc., who offer pro bono assistance to police agencies with unsolved cases gone cold. A case goes cold when detectives and law enforcement run out of leads. Frank was a member of the Vidocq Society. I was intrigued beyond words and wanted to learn more about the Jane Doe case and the Vidocq Society. Frank had ignited another flame in me that would influence my career for years. He was a great mentor and friend who I kept in touch with long after he left the Bensalem PD in 1997.

Sadly, Frank passed away from cancer on January 4, 2014. Through his influence, I am now a member of the Vidocq Society, and I try to do things the way he would. I think of him often and hope I would make him proud.

I was one of seven new officers Frank had hired at the Bensalem Police Department. Three of us had been assigned to the "Midnight Squad," a regular shift from 9:00 p.m. to 7:00 a.m. Our squad consisted of older veterans and "the rookies," as they liked to call us.

Dave Nieves was a young Puerto Rican kid from the projects in the Bronx. His family moved to Philadelphia after his brother was killed in a gang-related shooting. Dave was a natural, and after graduating from the police academy, was assigned as an undercover narcotics agent in a neighboring high school. He pulled off a genuine version of *21 Jump Street* and made quite an impressive name for himself. For the younger people reading this, I'm not referring to the movie version with Jonah Hill and Channing Tatum. The original *21 Jump Street* was a very popular police TV series that ran from 1987 through 1991. It starred actors Johnny Depp, Richard Grieco, and Holly Robinson Peete. After Nieves completed his assignment, he joined us on the midnight squad. To this day, he is one of the best street cops out there.

Then there was Christine Kelliher from Bucks County. She was a natural trainer with dogs and immediately gravitated toward becoming a K9 handler. Christine was an integral part of the DEA Task Force. Her work is responsible for some of the most significant drug and cash seizures in the history of the Bensalem Police. Somehow, we morphed her last name into "Cattle Herder." I don't recall who came up with that name, but it didn't matter because it stuck.

Most of us on the midnight squad had nicknames, and we even summoned one another via police radio by those names, or call signs, in those days. Don Kueny, "The Koon," was a Vietnam veteran and had been on the job since the mid-1970s. He was the king of one-liner jokes and acted like a tough guy, but inside, he was a softie. Don always looked after the younger members of the squad. On April 15, 1975, Bensalem Police Officer James K. Armstrong was shot and killed in the line of duty. He was a close friend of Don's, and on that date, every year, Don sat in his backyard and cried.

Greg Young, or "Youngs," was an Air Force veteran from Pittsburgh who loved Morris Day and his band The Time. He was always good for Morris Day quotes from the movie *Purple Rain*. Phil Stackhouse—"Steakhouse"—had been a Tastykake driver and loved to imitate "Porky Pig" from *Looney Tunes*. Kevin Lawler—"Kev"—was a Navy veteran and had survived the fire onboard the *USS Forrestal* in 1967. I was nicknamed "Mick," which was short for McMullin. Sadly, most of these guys are no longer with us, including Phil, Don, and, most recently, Greg. Greg passed away in 2020 from a long battle with cancer. Phil died from a heart attack; Don was very ill with emphysema and other complications; I miss them all.

Our supervisor was Sergeant Dale Richardson. To this day, I regard him as one of the best supervisors I've ever had. He was a no-nonsense, get-the-job-done kind of person. If you did the right thing, he would back you up. If you screwed up, he would tell you so, but he would help you correct it.

Our midnight squad was a melting pot of young and old, but we worked well together. We earned the name "Ratpack" from the 4 to 2 squad (4:00 p.m. to 2:00 a.m.) because we always backed each other up quickly, and they said we were like a bunch of rats scurrying around town. We wore the name like a badge of honor. No one accused the 4 to 2 squad of running calls as hard as we did. "The Koon" soon received another nickname from the Ratpack and became known as "Papa Rat."

On the night of January 4, 1995, I partnered with Officer Perry Ferrara, an excellent street cop who knew every street in his sector. The residents, at least the law-abiding ones, knew and loved him. It was a typical cold winter night. At 3:43 a.m., we responded to a burglary in progress at an apartment complex in the lower end of the township known as Andalusia. The dispatcher advised us that a large, bearded white male had broken through a ground-floor window at Station Ave. Apartments and was stealing items from the residence. He had been operating a white Honda Del Sol.

When we arrived at the apartment, we observed a white male getting into a white Del Sol, and we attempted to block him in with our vehicle. Perry got out and tried to pull the suspect from his car, but the guy was too big and strong. He started to drive away, dragging Perry, and struck our vehicle. I attempted to open his passenger door, but it was locked, so I tried to break the window. His car was still in motion, and things weren't working in our favor.

Perry got pinned between the suspect's car and a parked car, and I injured my back. The suspect drove off but made a U-turn and began heading toward us. I opened fire on him and his vehicle, firing six shots. The bullets hit his car, causing him to veer off and flee, which was better than trying to kill us. Sergeant Richardson, Dave, Greg, and Christine chased him down and caught him a few miles away. Perry and I were taken to the hospital and released later that day. We were banged up, but nothing too serious. The following month, I was brought before the shooting review board because I had violated our "Use of Force" policy by firing my weapon at a moving vehicle. Right before I walked into the conference room, a friend from Cherokee Day Camp contacted me and told me that another friend from our childhood camp had taken her own life.

This news put me in a bad mood for the Use of Force hearing. I think it showed in my demeanor when I responded to some of the stupid questions asked by the captain in charge of policies and procedures. As for my friend, her name was Mandy, and she died way too soon. Ultimately, I was cleared by the shooting review board due to "policy failure."

Unfortunately, the year 1995 continued to bring a series of unfortunate events. I was working the night shift on patrol and went home after finishing my shift around 8:15 a.m. Just as I lay down to sleep, the phone rang. My mom called to say that my cousin, Melissa, had just been found dead in Aunt Betsy's (Nan's sister) house. Melissa was Betsy's granddaughter. I had spoken to Melissa the previous week on the phone, arranging to give her some furniture for her new apartment that I no longer needed. I got up hurriedly and raced down to the Oxford Circle area of Philadelphia, where Aunt Betsy lived.

As I pulled up, I saw a Philadelphia Police car outside and approached the officer. I told him I was family and displayed my ID. He said it appeared to be a drug overdose, and a wagon was in route to transport the body to the medical examiner. I heard screaming and yelling as I started up the walkway to the house. I saw Nan at the front door, and she let me in. Melissa's lifeless body was lying on the living room floor, with Aunt Betsy sobbing beside her. I remember she was yelling for Melissa to wake up—she was mad at her for doing this to herself. She couldn't believe this had happened. I walked over to Aunt Betsy and helped her to her feet. Then I told Nan to take her and her husband, Uncle Pete, out of the house until the police removed Melissa's body. It was a stressful situation.

I needed a change after the shooting incident and Mandy's and Melissa's deaths. In 1996, a newly formed unit called the Community Policing Unit (CPU) had an opening, so I put in a memo requesting a transfer. The unit still proactively enforced the law, but the job also entailed community relations and events such as "Drug Abuse Resistance Education (D.A.R.E.)" and "problem-oriented policing," which necessitated identifying problems in the township and proactively addressing them. I was happy to start in the unit, and the change proved to be a good one.

I was asked to visit the kids at Cherokee Day Camp to do a little Q&A with them. Some of the best memories of my adolescence came from that very camp. Although I lived in Philadelphia, I had been a Cherokee camper during the summers of 1980-1984.

The summer of 1984 was my last season at Cherokee, but I worked as a counselor in training, or "CIT," as they were called. This position meant I was too old to be a camper but too young for employment. I assisted senior counselors in running their group activities for the day. We survived on Chef Boyardee, slapped-together peanut butter and jelly sandwiches, and Kool-Aid (they called it bug juice!), and we took weekly trips to the Rollerama skating rink. I used to love those trips because the kids would do their skating while I hung out with my friends. We listened to every hit song of the '80s played by the skating rink DJ. Whenever I hear a song by Asia, Journey, Rick Springfield, or Pat Benatar, it takes me back to those summer days. Corey Hart's hit song "Sunglasses at Night" made kids my age go out and buy Ray Ban sunglasses.

At camp, I had a friend named John who looked like a Ken doll and wore nothing but Ocean Pacific brand clothes with Ray Bans. There was also Debbie, who had a kick-ass boombox. That summer, she played nothing but Survivor's "Eye of the Tiger," "Round & Round" by Ratt, and Journey's *Frontiers* album on cassette.

A yellow merry-go-round near the water fountain was a gathering place for all the kids, and I remember sitting on it with friends while the boombox was blaring. My friend Ellen knew every word to every song, and to this day, I am still friends with her, John, and Debbie. Back then, *Transformers* was only an animated cartoon. Original movies like *The Karate Kid* and *Terminator* were among the most popular films. Who would have thought more than thirty years later there would be a television spin-off of *The Karate Kid* called *Cobra Kai?* Now if only I could get an acting audition for it!

My visit to Cherokee as a police officer went well, but it was bittersweet. I discovered that everyone who was part of the day camp staff in 1984 no longer worked there. It made me sad to think of how time had changed things. Stallone said it best in *Creed* when Rocky Balboa met Adonis Creed: "Time takes out everyone." It's true; you can't beat the clock.

Then there came one weird night in October 1997. I was driving along in my patrol car when an adult mallard duck appeared in the middle of the street. I tried to go around her, but she kept running in circles and wildly quacking to block the squad car. This mallard was going berserk! I finally got out of the car and followed the bird. I heard this loud chirping of baby ducks over to my left, and, at that point, I knew why the duck was going crazy. Her tiny ducklings had fallen through the heavy iron grate covering a storm drain near a pond and couldn't escape.

With the assistance of two other officers, I pried off the grate and reunited the feathery ducklings with their mother. *Weekly World News* was a newspaper sold mainly in supermarkets, and it got wind of the story. On October 14, 1997, it published a nationwide article titled *Distressed Duck Flags Down Police Car!*

Distressed duck flags down police car!

BENSALEM, Pa. — A hero mother duck saved her nine chicks from starvation — by flagging down a police car, then leading a puzzled cop to a storm drain where the baby birds were trapped!

"I had never seen anything like it," police officer Christopher McMullin told reporters.

Officer McMullin was driving along a quiet rural road when the frantic waterfowl hopped in front of the moving car.

The policeman tried to drive around the mallard, but it kept running around in circles to block the squad car, while quacking wildly. "It was going berserk," the officer said.

Finally, the confounded cop got out of the car and followed the bird.

"I hear this chirping of baby ducks over to my left — and now I know why the duck's going crazy," McMullin recalled.

The tiny birds had fallen through the heavy iron grate covering a storm drain near a pond and couldn't get out.

With the assistance of two other officers, McMullin pried off the grate and reunited the feathery family.

An ornithologist noted that the reasoning ability displayed by the duck is remarkable.

*P*ut all your eggs in one basket and WATCH THAT BASKET!

1997 Weekly World News article.
Credit: Weekly World News

The article told the story of a hero mother duck saving her nine ducklings from starvation by "flagging down a police car" and "leading a puzzled cop to a storm drain where the baby ducklings were trapped." Yes, the officer in that article was me. The story started as a joke within the police department. Still, it somehow caught the attention of this nationally known tabloid newspaper. Lucky me.

CHAPTER 3
Promotion

In 1998, I took the detective promotional exam. Out of every aspect of police work, being a detective was the position I was most interested in. I found mysteries fascinating and wanted to find answers and solve cases. My exam score was low, but I was still eligible for phase two of the process: an interview in front of a panel of police chiefs from other organizations. I didn't receive a stellar score in this phase either, but the average of the two scores got me on the detectives' list for promotion—that is, the very bottom of the list.

Being on the list meant that I had eighteen months of praying that enough promotions were made from the list to get down to me. After eighteen months, the list would expire, and if they hadn't gotten to me by then, I was out of the race and would have to test all over again. I was a bottom feeder, but I would take it. Several older guys retired during this period, and the list was moving.

It got down to about two months from the list expiration, and there were two of us left. The officer ahead of me on the list was Herb Laskow. He was a good guy, and we had gotten hired around the same time. Herb deserved the promotion. He was a good cop, intelligent, and had a college degree, which I did not. But about ten days before the list expired, Herb announced the FBI had hired him, and he was leaving the PD. I was more excited about him becoming an FBI agent than he was. That same week, another detective retired, creating a vacancy in the detective division. I was officially the sole bottom feeder on the promotion list, with ten days before expiration and one spot had become available.

The director of public safety was Steve Moran. Moran got approval from the township to fill the detective vacancy ahead of time and pushed my promotion through before the list expired. I must thank him again for looking out for me. In January 2000, just one day before the list expired, I was no longer the bottom feeder—I was the junior detective.

Shortly after my promotion, I found myself in the roll call room with several officers congratulating me and wishing me luck. Among those individuals stood Sergeant Bill Koszarek. But instead of congratulating me, he told me that I would've never been promoted in earlier times. He felt I didn't deserve the promotion and made no bones about it. He stated that in his generation, they would let the list die and test again to get the top-scoring candidates—whatever, he was entitled to his opinion.

After my promotion, I was assigned to the Criminal Investigations Division (CID). I worked with Dave Rouland frequently, and he conducted some excellent interviews I took part in. He had a deep, intimidating voice that was also soothing.

Whenever I arrived at work, Rouland would be outside smoking cigarettes in the parking lot, usually while talking with someone. I would joke around and say, "Is this guy ever working? Cause he's always outside smoking." But then, after a while, I realized he wasn't just taking cigarette breaks for himself—he was taking suspects outside to smoke while he conducted interviews with them. He was brilliant, and this approach offered a much less intimidating environment to get them to talk. A non-custodial interview allows you to talk with suspects willing to speak. It simply means that the individual has not been charged and is not in custody; they can end the interview and leave at any time.

During one robbery investigation we worked on together, Rouland and I linked two separate robberies to the same suspect and brought him into the PD for questioning. I was still very new and not confident in my interview skills, so Rouland took the reins and put the robbery suspect in the interview room. Within twelve minutes, he got a signed confession from the suspect and made an arrest. Rouland was good. He taught me a lot and did not share the same beliefs about me as Koszarek. In fact, Rouland was the exact opposite. He told me I was intuitive and encouraged me to follow my gut and instincts. Rouland retired about one year after my promotion.

My career as a detective continued to develop until March 2002. After several tests, I was diagnosed with a giant bone cell tumor in my left knee, fracturing my kneecap from underneath. I had to undergo surgery right away.

After the first six weeks of my recovery, I returned to work on light duty status. This meant I was allowed to hobble around on crutches, talk on the phone, and type up reports. But I couldn't do any investigations in the field. The status saved me from burning more of my sick time and allowed me to complete telephone-based interviews. I found myself bored out of my mind and searching for things to do. My supervisor, Sergeant Lois Kirgan, suggested I review a cold case file to keep me busy. She explained the case was an unsolved murder of a young teenage girl from the Trevose section of Bensalem in 1984. I wanted to look at it, but the file wasn't in the computer because it had never been entered into our new record-keeping system. After nagging Sergeant Kirgan enough times, she finally dug out several black binders for me. I began reading the files right away, and like a good book, I could not put it down.

While reviewing the original reports, several names stood out, including Detectives Koszarek, Rouland, and various other senior officers I knew. I was intrigued, and I took the case file home with me that night. The next day, I came to work and told Sergeant Kirgan I wanted to reopen the investigation. She smiled and said I could have it if I maintained my other cases.

The CID commander, Captain Robinson, overheard our conversation and asked, "Do you know who worked that case?" He indicated that some of the best investigators had worked on it and couldn't solve it. Robinson asked if I was sure I wanted to reopen it, and without hesitation, I answered, "Yes." He never really said it was okay to do, but he never overruled Sergeant Kirgan—so I kept the files. The case was solvable, in my opinion. The original detectives in 1984 did a great job, so I knew exactly where to start.

At this point, I still hadn't realized this was a case I had common ground with. It wasn't until a few weeks down the pike with the files that I came across an interview with a man named Hayes Biggs. Biggs was an employee at the Cherokee Day Camp, and it was at that moment I put it all together.

Memories of those Cherokee camp days as a young boy flooded me again. I began to recall one day when there was a lot of talk about a young girl in the neighborhood who had gone missing. Her name was Barbara Rowan. Although I came from Philadelphia, many Cherokee campers were locals from the Bensalem area, and some even knew her. Some insensitively joked that the "Neshaminy Devil" had gotten Barbara. The "Neshaminy Devil" is a rip-off version of the "Jersey Devil" folklore dating back to 1735. The "Jersey Devil" has been described as a kangaroo-like creature with short arms, the head of a dog, large bat wings, horns, and a pointed tail—very similar to a dragon, minus the fire breathing. According to the legend, the creature prowls through the marshes of Southern New Jersey, specifically the New Jersey Pinelands.

As for the "Neshaminy Devil," Cherokee Day Camp was built along the banks of the Neshaminy Creek, which feeds into the Delaware River, hence the name. Locals of all ages knew of the winged creature with hooves, a goat's head, bat-like wings, and a forked tail that growled and screamed before randomly attacking humans. It was just a typical campfire ghost story to scare campers. But the most unnerving feeling was passing by Barbara Rowan's house every day on the bus ride to and from camp.

I recalled the day Hayes Biggs' name was called over the camp PA system. Rumors quickly spread around camp that the police would arrest him and take him to jail. But that was only gossip, and the detectives were only there to question him about the missing girl because he knew her. None of us made the connection between Biggs and Barbara Rowan at the time. We were just dumb kids goofing off. I had forgotten about Barbara Rowan until I picked up the file 18 years after her murder.

Over the next couple of years, I repeatedly combed through the case files to familiarize myself with the investigation as much as possible. I started researching the key players, beginning with the main suspect in 1984, George Franz Shaw. I came to find out that he was still alive and living in Geneva, Florida. Another person of strong interest was Robert "Bobby" Sanders, who was also still alive and living in Stroudsburg, Pennsylvania.

As a matter of fact, all the original witnesses interviewed back in 1984 were still alive. Some still lived locally; some had moved away or were in prison. At that point, I decided not to contact the Rowan family because I didn't want to open old wounds and give them false hope. There were no guarantees I would solve the case. Some people disagreed with my decision, but I still stand by it.

CHAPTER 4
Barbara

Fourteen-year-old Barbara Rowan was reported missing by her father at 9:30 p.m. on August 3, 1984. She was an only child and lived with her parents, Robert and Patricia Rowan, in the Trevose section of Bensalem. Officer Albert Belardino was dispatched from the Bensalem Police and met Mr. and Mrs. Rowan outside their residence.

The Rowans lived modestly in a trailer park at the time. Her father last saw Barbara leaving the house earlier that day, wearing blue shorts with white stripes and a blue top with white trim. She had long, red hair, and blue eyes, stood five feet, six inches tall, and weighed 110 pounds.

She was carrying a softball with a glove and had a radio when she left. Robert Rowan told the officer that Barbara had a strict curfew of 7:00 p.m. and was never late. They were very concerned for their daughter.

Robert Rowan was an older Caucasian gentleman with a tall, thin build. His wife, Patricia, had red hair like her daughter and worked as a seamstress. By this time,

Barbara Rowan
Credit: Bensalem PD

Mr. Rowan had checked with most of Barbara's friends but couldn't locate her. Several neighbors were present and agreed that Barbara never stayed out past this time. On this night, however, she never returned home.

Upon questioning, Mr. Rowan stated they had moved several times in the past two years and had lived at different motels due to financial hardship. He denied any problems at home or arguments that may have taken place with Barbara earlier that day.

The officer reported that Mr. Rowan was visibly upset and choked up with emotion several times while giving his report. Mr. Rowan made it a point to say that, although his daughter was fourteen years old physically, she was several years behind in maturity and mainly played with younger children. Barbara had left home at around 3:30 in the afternoon without mentioning where she was going. This was not uncommon, according to her mother.

Neighbors last saw Barbara walking south on Old Lincoln Highway. The officer explained to the Rowans that police would check the area to try to locate their daughter. If they couldn't find her and she still did not return, they would file a missing person's affidavit, where police would enter Barbara into the National Crime Information Center (NCIC), and then they would give more attention to the matter. Officer Belardino patrolled the neighborhood and surrounding streets that evening in an attempt to locate Barbara, but the young teen did not turn up.

Two days later, on August 5, Barbara was entered into NCIC as a missing juvenile. Detective Moran interviewed Barbara's mother. She told Moran that her daughter had never run away before and denied any implications of a family dispute involving Barbara. She admitted that for a short time, while Barbara was in seventh grade, her sister, Barbara's aunt, Ruth Zielinski, had had custody of her so she could attend school.

Patricia Rowan last saw her daughter at approximately 3:30 p.m. on August 3, when she left their trailer. She recalled the events of that day, stating Mr. Rowan was at work and returned home somewhere between 6:30 and 6:45 p.m. that evening. About thirty minutes later, at approximately 7:15 p.m., Robert Rowan noticed Barbara had still not returned home. Still, he and his boss, Robert Marschall, left and drove to a local bar called the Sandpiper Inn to get something to eat.

At that time, Patricia Rowan began to drive around the area and look for Barbara. She stopped at a house she described as red in color, just south of the trailer park on Old Lincoln Highway. The locals called it "the red house," consisting of three separate apartments in the front and two in the back. The rear apartments were believed to be vacant at the time. The front apartments on the left and right were ground level. The center apartment was a second-floor unit.

2019, the red house is no longer red;
George Shaw's apartment on the far left

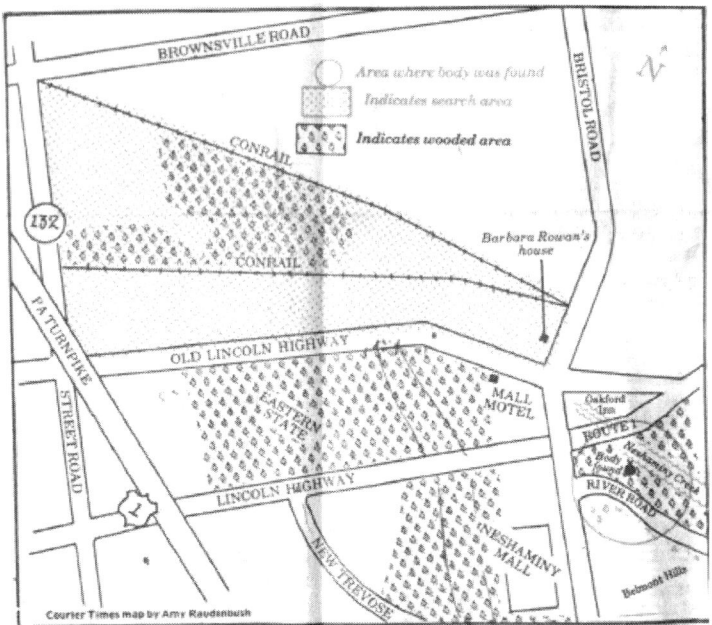

This map depicts the location of Barbara Rowan's home in relation to the Mall Motel, Old Lincoln Highway, and the red house

There, she knocked on the door and spoke to the resident in the first apartment, who was identified as Kevin Clark, a twenty-five-year-old Caucasian male. Clark occupied the first apartment of the red house closest to the trailer park where the Rowans lived. It appeared the young man was alone inside the apartment. He told Mrs. Rowan he had not seen their daughter.

Robert Rowan drank one beer at the Sandpiper Inn. He wanted to leave because he was concerned about his daughter's whereabouts. He and his boss left the bar shortly after, and upon his return home, he and his wife searched the neighborhood together. At approximately 10:30 p.m., Mr. Rowan returned to the red house and knocked on the middle apartment door with no answer. The third door, believed to be that of George Shaw, was answered by a man, at which time Mr. Rowan held up a photo of Barbara and asked if he had seen her, but the answer was no. Mr. Rowan gave police an account of his whereabouts on August 3, substantiated during an interview with Marschall.

On August 5, Robert Rowan searched the wooded lot behind the Mall Motel and later met with Officer William Fox. He turned in several items he had found in the lot, including a record album, claiming it to be Barbara's. He insisted he had purchased the same record album for Barbara one week before at the flea market. The items were labeled and stored as evidence. The Nottingham Town Watch Association was also searching the woods. By the end of the day, Robert Rowan began to grow frustrated because of the lack of attention this incident was receiving from both the press and the police.

Over the next forty-eight hours, zero leads turned up, despite the efforts of organized police and helicopter searches. Detectives Koszarek and Rouland were assigned to the missing juvenile's case. The Bensalem Police worked relentlessly, interviewing neighborhood residents and employees of a nearby auto shop and motel. However, time passed, and the officers still found no leads or tangible evidence.

Detectives pressed forward and interviewed neighbor and friend James Frederickson. He was a twenty-year-old white male. Frederickson told Moran that he and Barbara had played catch in front of his trailer on August 3. She abandoned their game of catch and left the trailer park at approximately 3:40 p.m. Barbara told him she was going to see her coach and was carrying a glove, a ball, and a radio. When Barbara left the trailer park, she was walking toward Old Lincoln Highway, Frederickson claimed. He wasn't aware that she had ever played on a softball team. And he said that was the last time he saw her.

Deborah Pudder, a twenty-three-year-old white female, managed the archery range on Old Lincoln Highway and was with her younger sister Danette (age ten) on August 3. In her interview with detectives, Deborah stated she left her sister alone at the archery range at around 4:00 p.m. and returned approximately thirty minutes later. Upon Deborah's return, Danette told her she had heard a radio playing. When she looked out the office window, Danette had observed Barbara Rowan walking down Old Lincoln Highway, playing her radio. During this time, two male subjects approached the office steps, whispered something to each other, then turned around and walked toward the girl she believed to be Barbara. Danette described the girl she saw as having long, red hair, glasses, blue shorts, and possibly a purple-colored top. The two males were described as approximately twenty years old, white, very dirty, and both had black or dark brown hair. Deborah had observed them hanging around in the area for about a week and said they were filthy and appeared to be living on the streets.

Jessie Disney, a fifteen-year-old female who resided at the Mall Motel with her mother, was interviewed. She told detectives that Barbara was more of an acquaintance than her friend. Disney described Barbara as a loner who experienced problems with kids on her school bus and in the trailer park and who didn't have many friends. The last time she had seen Barbara was about two to three weeks prior. Disney ran into Barbara at around 2:30 p.m. at the Mall Motel with an unfamiliar man. She described the man as rough-looking, in his early twenties, about five feet, ten inches tall, heavyset, with dark-colored hair and a beard. Disney recalled that Barbara and the man appeared friendly to each other, but they were not holding hands. Barbara had introduced him to Disney, but she could not remember his name.

Al's Used Auto Parts is a business located right across the street from the red house at 4400 Old Lincoln Highway. Al Gougler was and still is the owner of the company, as well as the owner/landlord of the red house. One of Gougler's employees, Joe Snow, had been renting the upstairs front apartment with his girlfriend, Cecelia Biggs. As previously described, the downstairs front apartment on the left was rented to Shaw. Shaw was described as a white male, approximately thirty years old, five feet, nine inches tall, with a stocky build. Shaw was unemployed and had previously approached Snow about obtaining drugs, according to Gougler. He occupied the apartment with his wife and young daughter. Gougler had recently witnessed Shaw vacuuming his car's trunk.

According to an interview with Snow on August 7, Barbara told him she had been babysitting for the people below him, indicating the Shaws' apartment. Reportedly, Shaw had been residing in the apartment for approximately one month. His daughter, Kelly, was about three years old. At about 5:30 p.m. on August 3, Barbara was at Snow's apartment with his girlfriend, Cecelia Biggs, and her brother, Hayes Biggs.

Hayes did not reside in the apartment with Snow and his sister and was an employee at the Cherokee Day Camp. Snow told detectives that Barbara was at Shaw's apartment almost daily. He wasn't sure if she babysat for them, but he often saw her playing with Kelly.

Detective Terry Lachman observed a black and gold Chevrolet Impala parked in front of the apartment. The vehicle belonged to Shaw, according to Snow. Cecelia told detectives she last saw Barbara on Friday, August 3, at approximately 5:00 in the evening. She was hanging around in the parking lot outside their apartment. She told Cecelia she was there to babysit for Shaw, but Shaw was not home then, and Barbara had been waiting in the parking lot since 4:00 p.m.

She came to their apartment and played with their dog for about fifteen minutes, then left to check if Shaw had returned home. Cecelia informed investigators that Hayes had also spoken to Barbara that afternoon. Barbara told him Shaw had asked her to watch their daughter, Kelly. When Cecelia learned that Barbara had gone missing, she confronted Shaw about the girl. He denied having seen her that day.

Shaw was first interviewed on the morning of August 7 by Detective Lachman at Shaw's residence. He was wearing glasses and had a mustache. Shaw told detectives he had last seen Barbara on Friday, August 3, upon his return home from dropping his wife off at work. Barbara was out front and played with his daughter until approximately 5:30 p.m. and then visited the upstairs neighbors. A short time later, he observed her leaving. Barbara told him she had to return the radio she had with her to her friend but did not give a name. Shaw said she was carrying a radio, a baseball glove, and a softball.

When asked how often Barbara was at his apartment, Shaw stated she had come over to play with his daughter three to four times over about one month. He and his wife, Lori, had previously discussed Barbara babysitting their daughter, but both had agreed she was too young. His wife worked in Horsham, Pennsylvania, and on August 3, George drove his wife to work at approximately 3:00 p.m. According to his statement, George and his daughter lay down for a nap after Barbara returned home. He and Kelly met his wife at work for lunch at around 8:00 p.m.

The next stop for detectives was Cherokee Day Camp—the place of Hayes' employment. Hayes was described as a white male in his twenties and over six feet tall with dark hair. He recalled that on August 3, just after 4:00 p.m., he went to his sister Cecelia's apartment. Barbara was out front and told Hayes she was waiting for the downstairs neighbor to return home so she could babysit. She was expecting him to return between 4:30 and 5:00 p.m. He observed George Shaw's return home a short time later. Hayes left the apartment with his sister at approximately 6:30 that evening to attend a birthday party. At that time, he heard Barbara laughing inside Shaw's apartment. Hayes believed she was playing with Shaw's daughter. He didn't see Shaw's car at the apartment at that time but said it could have been parked in the back of the building.

Hayes told detectives that Barbara confessed she kept her babysitting for Shaw a secret from her parents because her mother did not want her taking care of anyone else's children. Her parents believed she was too immature to handle the responsibility.

Later that day, detectives visited Barbara's parents again. On the day she went missing, Barbara had told neighbors she was going to see her softball coach. But Mr. and Mrs. Rowan stated Barbara did not play for any teams, and they could not think of who she may have been referring to as a "coach" or where that person may live.

Robert and Patricia Rowan told police that their daughter had not been babysitting for anyone. They admitted Barbara had often asked them if she could babysit, but they would not let her because they felt she was too young and immature. Upon further questioning, the radio Barbara had been carrying around with her on the day she went missing was her own and not that of a friend, according to the Rowans.

The radio ownership proved to be another inconsistency with Shaw's statement. Why would Barbara tell him she had to return the radio to a friend when it was hers? When questioned about any friends their daughter played with, Mr. and Mrs. Rowan named Jimmy (James Frederick), Disney, and some other friends who owned a horse and lived on Old Lincoln Highway, just before the archery range. They confirmed she was last seen wearing blue jogging shorts with white stripes, a blue tank top with white trim, and blue sandals.

On that same day, investigators spoke to Peggy Dornish, manager of the Mall Motel. Her sixteen-year-old son Chuck was friends with Barbara. According to an interview with Chuck, he last saw Barbara on Friday, August 3, at approximately 10:45 a.m. He stated she was alone at the time and was looking for Disney. He observed her carrying a baseball and glove but did not know where she went from there.

The investigation continued, and on August 7 and 8, the Bensalem Police searched the wooded areas around the Bridges Trailer Park and other surrounding parts with the assistance of a Pennsylvania State Police helicopter, numerous volunteer fire companies, and a trained bloodhound dog. Frustratingly and disappointingly, the searches turned up nothing. By this time, Barbara's photo had been released and aired on all the local TV news stations. Police had distributed flyers of Barbara's photo all along U.S. Route 1 and at multiple retail and business locations.

The police interviewed Shaw again, this time at the Bensalem Township Police Department. Detectives

Lachman and William Klosz conducted this interview. Shaw told detectives that Barbara had come to his apartment on August 2 and 3. He said Barbara had not been around for about one and a half weeks before those visits. Barbara told Shaw she had been away visiting relatives or friends.

Shaw claimed that Barbara arrived at the apartment around noon on August 3, and his wife and daughter were home with him. Barbara was in and out of the apartment playing with Kelly. At approximately 3:15 p.m., Shaw took his wife to work at Decision Data Computer Corporation in Horsham. Kelly went with them. According to Shaw, Barbara was in the driveway when they left their apartment. Shaw and his daughter returned home at around 4:30 p.m., and he observed Barbara talking to Cecelia. After parking his car around the back and walking to the front of his apartment, Cecelia had already gone inside. Barbara came around the building to meet him and Kelly, Shaw claimed. Then they entered the apartment, and Barbara and Kelly began playing.

Shaw told detectives that a short time later, at approximately 6:00 p.m., he was doing the dishes when two strangers came by the apartment. Shaw described them as white, one male and one female, both in their twenties. The couple was later revealed as Timmy Johnson and his girlfriend, Holly Shaeffer. They were inquiring about a Ford Falcon that Snow had for sale. Barbara and Kelly were playing outside when Shaw came to the door and spoke to Johnson and Shaeffer. He believed Cecelia had left her apartment by then because her car was no longer there.

After the two individuals left, so did Barbara. Shaw said Barbara told him she had to return the radio she had to a friend and left his apartment shortly after 6:00 p.m. He recalled Barbara also had a baseball glove and softball in hand. After she left, Shaw said he put Kelly down for a nap and then lay on the couch in the living room, where he fell asleep. He set his alarm for 7:50 p.m. to wake up and get ready to meet Lori for lunch at her job. Lori's lunch break was from 8:30 to 9:00 p.m. every evening.

Shaw claimed that when the alarm went off, he got up, put Kelly in the car, and drove to his wife's place of work in Horsham. On the night of August 3, he brought his wife tacos. Then he returned to their apartment with Kelly at about 9:30 or 9:45 p.m. Shaw said he was bathing his daughter when Mr. Rowan knocked on the door and asked if he had seen Barbara or knew where she was. Shaw told Mr. Rowan she had been there earlier but had left to return a friend's radio and did not know the friend's name. "Barbara was always trying to babysit or sell one of her toys," claimed Shaw. But she was never allowed to babysit their daughter because he and his wife felt she was too young.

When questioned about leaving Barbara alone with his daughter, he insisted she was never allowed to watch Kelly alone. Shaw claimed he met Barbara about one week after he and his family moved into the apartment around July 1 and that she had been there approximately

five times since. He told detectives that they did not see
Barbara right after the Fourth of July for about one and
a half weeks. In Shaw's previous statement, he said he
believed they had not seen her for one and a half weeks
before August 2. Detectives caught on to this discrepancy.

The detectives asked Shaw to take a polygraph exam,
and he agreed to it, but only if his wife could be with
him. Police told him that he had to take the exam alone.
He told detectives he wanted to further discuss the matter
with his wife before committing. He was supposed to
contact them the following day to schedule the polygraph
but never did.

That same day, Johnson contacted detectives and
stated he had gone to Snow's apartment about a car for
sale on Friday, August 3. It was approximately 5:30 p.m.,
but no one answered at the Snow residence. He noticed
a white Chevrolet Nova (believed to be Snow's vehicle)
in front of the house when a young girl came out of the
downstairs apartment on the left and introduced herself as
Barbara. A white male with a mustache and glasses (Shaw)
approached the door and told him that Snow had already
sold the car. Barbara appeared to be playing at the Shaw
residence and was all right, stated Johnson. When asked
by police who was with him at the time, Johnson said his
girlfriend, Holly Shaeffer, was there.

For the next few days, hundreds of phone calls flooded
the Bensalem Police Department with reported sightings
of females matching Barbara's description. The alleged
sightings ran anywhere from highway hitchhikers to bus

stations, malls, train stations, and even airports all over the tri-state area. Unfortunately, none of these reports turned up anything tangible. But the phone calls continued to pour in, and past affiliates and neighbors of Robert and Patricia Rowan contacted detectives with a growing number of damaging statements. Several of those reports disclosed alleged physical and mental abuse by Mr. and Mrs. Rowan toward Barbara. As time passed, talk on the street stirred up. The public eye began pointing fingers at Robert Rowan, claiming that Barbara likely ran away to escape her abusive parents. None of these allegations were ever substantiated.

The police department received a phone call from an unidentified female claiming to be a psychic. She reported the little girl, fourteen years old, missing from Old Lincoln Highway, was being held against her will in a rose-colored trailer in the trailer park across from the Mall Motel (the same trailer park where Barbara was from). She stated a white, middle-aged male living alone in the trailer kidnapped the girl and that the girl was terrified and being kept under a bed where the man was feeding her dirty scraps of food. Although the psychic revealed he did not abuse the girl, she said the man would "kill the girl in two days." Police identified the trailer, and when they arrived and knocked on the door, a man described as "eccentric" allowed them in. They searched and found nothing.

During an interview, nearby resident Jim Pendergast told detectives that Barbara had come by and asked him for $5 about two weeks prior. Barbara had been trying to collect money to buy a special birthday present for someone. She told him that Shaw owed her the money for babysitting. Pendergast felt sorry for her and gave her the money. He also bought a toy she was selling for $2.

That same day on August 8, Rosemary Capirchio, a guidance counselor at the Schafer Elementary School, was interviewed regarding her knowledge of Barbara. Capirchio had been Barbara's counselor during the past school year and knew her reasonably well. She described Barbara as having very few friends. She explained that she was not a "slow" person, as had been previously communicated to the police by other sources. However, she stated that Barbara was obsessed with being popular and accepted by her peers. She was not well-received by her age group, and consequently, Barbara tended to cling to adults or younger children.

In reference to Barbara's home life, Capirchio could not supply much information. However, she did indicate that Barbara was afraid of her father. Capirchio referred to an incident immediately before the end of the school year, where she spoke to Barbara regarding the possibility of failing. Barbara had to pass the year's final test to proceed to the next grade level; therefore, Capirchio told Barbara she would contact her parents to advise them of the situation. Barbara was terrified, and throughout the day, she pleaded with Capirchio not to call her parents due to the harsh repercussions she expected from her father.

Detectives at the Bensalem PD questioned Robert Rowan about his disciplining of Barbara. Mr. Rowan considered the discipline he enforced on Barbara as "standard." However, he admitted to hitting her occasionally when he felt it necessary. He denied using any punishment, including hitting Barbara, in the week before her disappearance. According to Robert, even if Barbara had been afraid to tell her parents something, she would have still come home despite any punishment she may receive. Investigators checked with Bucks County Children and Youth Services regarding the Rowan family. They found no records of open cases or substantiated abuse.

W.C. Presley Jr. was also a Bridges Trailer Park resident. Presley told detectives that he had known Barbara for about six months and thought highly of her. He described her as almost one of his own children. However, he admitted he had teased Barbara about her "relationship" with Jimmy Frederickson, e.g., a boyfriend-girlfriend situation. "But she did not seem bothered by that at all," Presley stated. He claimed he had last seen Barbara just before 3 p.m. on Friday, August 3, playing ball in the driveway with Frederickson. He had overheard Frederickson going into his trailer to check the time and telling Barbara it was three minutes to 3:00, and he wanted to go inside to watch something on television. Presley did not see Barbara or Frederickson anymore that day, but he did tell detectives that Barbara had eaten at his trailer earlier in the day, along with Presley's three children and another young girl whom his wife babysat. Detectives gave Presley a polygraph exam, which he passed without question.

Norman Rowan, Barbara's uncle, visited police headquarters on August 10, concerned about the investigation of the disappearance of his niece. Norman had heard several things around the trailer park that confused him and was looking for clarification. Norman and Robert did not have the best relationship, and he attested to Robert's temper when he drank. When Norman first saw the news report, he thought Barbara had run away, knowing how strict Robert was in raising her. He told police that Robert was upset with how the investigation was going and that he reported that police had "interrogated" him and his wife at the police station for over four hours. According to Norman, Robert felt that the police were focusing on him as if he was hiding Barbara or had killed her himself.

Ruth Zielinski, Patricia Rowan's sister, last saw Barbara on August 1 at the Roosevelt Flea Market with her mother. Zielinski told detectives that Barbara had lived with her for approximately six months in 1981 while the Rowans resided in Philadelphia. Barbara was perfect while staying with her and got along well with her two daughters, Jackie and Linda, then twelve and fourteen years of age. Ruth had never seen or heard the Rowans abuse Barbara but admitted that Barbara would sometimes get mouthy with her mom and scream and yell like she was being hurt when she really wasn't. Zielinski added that if Barbara ever had any problems she could not discuss with her parents, she would call her to discuss them. Zielinski was unaware of any issues Barbara may have been having at home. Zielinski said she was not very close with her sister and would only see or talk to her once every few weeks; therefore, she didn't know much about their personal lives. She described Barbara as a friendly girl and said she would stop and talk to anyone, especially if they had an animal with them. Zielinski continued that Barbara had told her daughters approximately two months prior that she had a boyfriend named Scott White (seventeen years old) and had met him when she went to school in Morrisville. Zielinski explained that it was typical for Barbara to copy something she heard one of her daughters say. For example, if one of her daughters said she had a boyfriend, Barbara would create a fictitious boyfriend of her own. Zielinski didn't think Barbara would get into a car with a stranger, but if someone asked for directions, she would get close and talk to them. She also didn't believe Barbara would run away.

On August 13, detectives visited Shaw at his home for a third interview. This time, they focused on the clothing worn by Barbara the day she went missing. He could not give any information concerning her attire that day and stated it didn't seem important to him then.

CHAPTER 5
Finding Barbara

On August 16, 1984, David Watkins was searching for his missing dog along North River Drive, less than a half mile from Barbara's home, when he discovered a decomposed body lying face down in a heavily wooded area on the side of the road, approximately twelve feet west of North River Drive and forty feet north of a utility pole. U.S. Route 1, a heavily traveled highway, is around fifteen to twenty feet west of North River Drive and visible from where Watkins found the remains. Route 1 runs parallel to some portions of North River Drive, with the wooded area separating the two roads. Someone could have easily pulled off to the shoulder of Route 1 and discreetly dumped the victim's body into the wooded brush.

Watkins notified the police, and Officer Fox was the first officer on the scene, followed by Officers Knowles, Thompson, and Maddocks. Once there, they secured the crime scene.

**Photo of the 1984 crime scene on North River Drive.
Credit: Bensalem PD**

**Present day photo where Barbara Rowan's
body was found in 1984
Credit: Maria Viola Jefferson**

Detectives photographed the scene and surrounding area while waiting for the coroner to arrive. Detective Koszarek came first, followed by Deputy Coroner John

McGlone and Detective Frank Dykes of the Bucks County District Attorney's Office. They took more photos, along with items of investigative value. The police cut back the brush and weeds to expose the victim's body better. The location of her body was about a half mile from Shaw's home.

The body was in an advanced state of decomposition and had no recognizable features aside from a small amount of shoulder-length red hair on top of the skull and a partially matching description of Barbara's clothing on the last day she was seen: a blue shirt with white trim. The body was unclothed from the waist down. The decedent's red hair, partial attire, and height suggested the remains were those of Barbara Rowan. Someone had bound her hands, ankles, and mouth with black duct tape.

The following day, forensic pathologist Dr. Halbert Fillinger performed an autopsy. Dr. Fillinger determined the remains to be those of a white female in her teens in a severely decomposed state. The majority of the remains were skeletal. Whoever killed her had wrapped tape around her neck, mouth, and skull area. Per Dr. Fillinger, this suggested she had died of suffocation. The tape was approximately two inches wide, black, and had a cloth base. Her hands had been bound behind her back with a cellophane-type tape. This tape had an unusual fiber running lengthwise approximately one inch wide. The killer had also wrapped the same tape around the victim's feet and ankles. Dr. Fillinger ruled the death a homicide by asphyxiation. The identification was made official using dental records and a comparison of the decedent's hair with samples taken from a hairbrush belonging to Barbara.

In interviews later that day, neighbors along North River Drive reported a rank odor, as if a dead animal had been lingering in the area for the past few weeks.

Diane Watkins, the wife of David, who discovered the body on North River Drive, called detectives with an interesting account. She and her husband now remembered that, one day during the previous week, she had seen a dark green four-door 1974 Chevrolet Impala, described as "beat up-looking," that had been parked on North River Drive, right where the body was found. It was unoccupied and had remained there for two days before vanishing. She had assumed it was disabled.

Alan James Miller was a ten-year-old boy at the time and also lived in the Bridges Trailer Park community with his parents. During his interview on August 17, Alan told police he saw Barbara Rowan on Wednesday, August 1, when he and Barbara played catch in the driveway of the trailer park. According to Alan, Barbara became upset when the ball accidentally went into the Millers' garden. She insisted she had to get the ball to practice with her coach. However, Alan's mother would not let him retrieve the ball until his father came home. Alan returned the ball to Barbara the next day after his father recovered it.

When asked in further reference to the coach, Alan added that he asked Barbara what her coach's name was, and she replied that she couldn't tell him. Then he asked if her mother knew she was seeing a coach, and Barbara answered, "No." She said her mother knew nothing about it. Barbara asked Alan if he wanted to go to the red house with her, but his mother would not let him. According to Alan, she never mentioned anyone by the name of George.

Barbara and Alan usually played outside until Mr. Miller returned home from work at approximately 4:00–4:30 p.m. when Alan would go inside for dinner. On the evening of August 1, Barbara stayed at the Miller residence for dinner, asking Mrs. Miller to let her know when it was almost 7:00 p.m. Mrs. Miller alerted Barbara at 6:55 p.m., and Barbara left for home. Mr. Miller then interjected that Barbara almost always abided by her curfew of 7:00 p.m. and that she was not one to wander. Alan added that the only places Barbara ever went to were the Mall Motel and the red house.

Alan denied any conversations between him and Barbara about her babysitting. However, he did say that, on at least two occasions, Barbara had picked up Kelly and brought her to the trailer park after she had asked Jennifer and Denise Presley if they wanted to play with her.

Alan observed Barbara on Friday afternoon, August 3, sitting by a pole in front of a nearby trailer, throwing a ball in the air. "She was quiet at that time," he said. Then Frederickson came out of his trailer and began playing ball with Barbara in the driveway, so Alan went into his house and never saw Barbara again.

The Bensalem Police worked the homicide case hard and narrowed down the potential list of suspects. At this point, they homed in on George Shaw.

On August 18, 1984, a fourth interview with Shaw was conducted at the Bensalem PD, and Detectives Koszarek and Scar advised him of his rights. Shaw stated he had first seen Barbara at around noon on August 3. He told them that Barbara had played with Kelly until approximately 3:20 p.m., when he and Kelly had to leave to take his wife, Lori, to work. Reportedly, Shaw drove his beige Chevy, and Barbara was standing in the driveway when they left.

Upon returning home from dropping his wife off at work at approximately 4:30 p.m., Shaw observed Barbara waiting outside their apartment. He told detectives that Barbara played with Kelly for a little while, then left his apartment at approximately 6:00 that evening with her radio, baseball, and glove. He then put Kelly down for a nap, and when he woke her up at 8:00 p.m., they both left in a hurry to meet his wife for lunch at her place of work. Decision Data was about a thirty-five-minute drive from Shaw's residence.

They arrived at her workplace around 8:30 p.m., but he couldn't remember if they stayed there or went out to eat. Having lunch with his wife had been his routine since getting laid off sixteen weeks prior, Shaw explained. He and Kelly left his wife's job at 9:00 p.m. then stopped in Hatboro to talk to a couple of friends by the McDonald's. They returned home around 10:00 p.m., when he got Kelly's bath ready, and they both remained awake watching television. His wife's shift ended at 12:30 a.m., so at 11:50 p.m., he and Kelly left again to pick his wife up from work. Shaw estimated they got home at 1:15–1:30 in the morning at the latest.

The inconsistencies with Shaw's interview just ten days prior drew further suspicion. During the interview on August 7, Shaw had reported going to Taco Bell in Southampton and picking up some food that he took to his wife's place of work and ate there, compared with not remembering what they ate during this particular interview. He had also told Detective Lachman that he had gone right home after eating lunch at his wife's workplace at about 9:30–9:45 p.m. When detectives questioned him about his previous statement, Shaw insisted that his account about going to the Hatboro McDonald's and talking to some friends after having lunch with his wife was, in fact, correct.

Additionally, on August 7, Shaw had reported that he was getting Kelly's bath ready when Mr. Rowan came to his house and asked if he had seen Barbara or knew where she had gone. Yet, Shaw did not mention Robert Rowan coming to the apartment during this interview.

Shaw insisted that he had never asked Barbara to babysit for him; however, he admitted she had taken Kelly to the swings at the trailer park several times. According to Shaw, Barbara would ask to babysit for him all the time and was constantly trying to sell toys and things to make money, either to pay someone back or to buy a present for someone's birthday. He also said he did not remember seeing Barbara on August 2, contradictory to his previous interview statement on August 7.

On this same day, August 7, detectives met with Lori Ann Shaw, George's wife. Detectives Koszarek and Dykes conducted the interview. Lori worked as a computer assembler. Her usual work schedule was Monday through Friday on the second shift, 4:00 p.m. to 12:30 a.m. She left the house at approximately 3:15 p.m. for her commute.

According to Lori, George had last worked for C & W Industries in Southampton, Pennsylvania as a "plater," which involved welding or bolting construction plates together. He was with this company for almost one year before being laid off in February 1984. George had been home during the daytime collecting unemployment since they moved to the Old Lincoln Highway apartment on July 1, 1984. Before working at C&W Industries, he worked for Ruch's Tool Company in Willow Grove, Pennsylvania, for approximately two years but was eventually laid off there too.

Lori told detectives that she and her husband owned two vehicles, including the black-over-gold Chevrolet (parked outside at the time of the interview) and a white and red 1971 Pontiac LeMans Sport, which had been unusable since breaking down about a month before. She told detectives that the disabled vehicle was in a parking lot somewhere on 2nd Street Pike in nearby Southampton, although this was never confirmed, and the car was never located. They had also owned an old 1967 Buick Skylark, which they junked.

According to the original testimonials, George had been driving his wife to work for weeks because they only had one operational vehicle. And since Lori's father had been recently injured in an auto accident, leaving him incapacitated, George had been going to her father's house to help him with chores and yard work while Lori was at work.

When questioned whether Barbara Rowan had ever done any babysitting for them, Lori told detectives that Barbara had offered the first couple of times they met, but she never took Barbara up on it. However, she let Barbara take Kelly to the trailer park to play with some kids on at least one occasion. Otherwise, Lori was adamant that she never discussed using Barbara as a babysitter with George.

Lori knew that Barbara had been to their apartment several times before meeting her. Lori also believed Barbara had been there about three or four times during their first week there. But then Lori hadn't seen her for two weeks and assumed Barbara and her family were away. When Barbara returned the following week, she visited their apartment twice weekly, on average. Lori knew Barbara visited more often after she left for work, when George was with Kelly, to keep her occupied.

She had not seen Barbara on August 3 and could not specifically remember when she had last seen Barbara. She recalled George took her to work between 3:15 p.m. and 3:30 p.m., and Barbara had not been there before they left. According to Lori, it was common practice for George to bring food and meet her at work on her lunch break at 8:30 p.m. She told detectives that he did this on the evening of August 3. She first learned Barbara had gone missing after work that same night when George told her Mr. Rowan had been looking for her.

Lori said she had discouraged her husband from taking a polygraph test. She believed too many things could falsely affect the results, and although she was fine taking one herself, she thought that George was too much of a nervous type to guarantee total accuracy.

According to Lori's accounts, her husband had never mentioned Barbara being in their apartment after 7:00 p.m. on August 3, nor could she recall what time George told her Barbara had left that evening. She was never sure where Barbara lived precisely, but she knew she lived in the trailer park. Lori added that their daughter Kelly routinely went to bed late, slept in late, and never took a nap in between, except when in the car. She was often asleep in the car when George picked Lori up from work.

CHAPTER 6
Bobby Sanders Is The Key

A detailed police timeline traced Barbara's whereabouts from witness accounts on August 3, 1984. Robert Rowan told police there had been a second guy—presumably Robert "Bobby" Sanders—at the apartment on the night of August 3 when he knocked on Shaw's door looking for her.

Robert Romanski told the original investigators that he saw Shaw at the McDonald's on York Road at approximately 8:00–8:30 p.m. on the night of August 3, 1984. In 2004, Sanders gave a similar account to Detective Mike Mosiniak and me. According to Sanders, he had left the McDonald's with Shaw and rode with him to his apartment, although he was unsure of the time. In 1984, Shaw had told detectives he was having lunch with his wife at her work at the same time.

Shaw had previously claimed he and Kelly had returned home at 10:00 at night, and Mr. Rowan had shown up at his apartment around 10:30 looking for Barbara. He left Sanders out of the entire equation as if he had never been with them. But Sanders admitted to us in 2004 that he had been inside the apartment and witnessed a frantic Robert Rowan searching for his daughter.

The Bensalem PD tip line received and recorded a phone call from an anonymous caller on August 18, stating his friends were involved in the murder in Bensalem. No names were given, but the caller was noticeably upset on the phone. The caller also singled out one particular friend, who told him if he ever told anyone, he would hurt him. A verbatim transcription of the phone call went as follows:

"Him and his buddies, he didn't mean to hurt that girl, Barb Rowan, and I, and he said if I said anything, he gonna hurt me. And I just wanted somebody to know about it."

Shortly after, the individual abruptly terminated the call, and the recording was placed with the case file.

Two days later, on August 20, Michelle Green called the police to report some information she believed could be helpful in the Barbara Rowan murder case. On August 3, she and her husband were driving north on Route 1 in Bensalem at approximately 8:30 p.m. when they observed a vehicle on the east shoulder of the highway across from the Oakford Inn.

Mrs. Green explained that the car was stopped where the guardrail began, and a man stood next to the open trunk. The same individual was removing an item, wrapped in white, that could have been a body from the trunk. In addition, Mrs. Green observed what appeared to be blue-colored flip-flops on the shoulder of the road, below the vehicle's license plate. Much later, this tip would serve as a turning point in the Barbara Rowan murder case. Mrs. Green described the individual as a white male with a medium build and slightly muscular with dirty blond hair and wearing an odd painter's-like cap that was very dirty.

Her husband, Danny Green, explained that he and his wife were driving northbound on Route 1 in the evening hours. He wasn't sure about the exact time but said it was getting dark outside. Just across from what was then the Sandpiper Bar (more recently known as the Oakford Inn), he observed a car stopped on the side of the road with the trunk open. There was a man who looked like he was picking something white or light-colored up out of the trunk. Mr. Green described the person he saw as a thirty- to thirty-five-year-old white male, six feet tall, muscular, with dark hair and black-rimmed eyeglasses, wearing either dark blue jeans or work pants and a dark-colored shirt. The car possibly had an old Pennsylvania plate (yellow background with blue letters).

Michael Ockford was a twenty-nine-year-old white male and the roommate of Kevin Clark, who lived in the right-side ground apartment on the front of the red house. He had lived at that residence for seven years. According to Michael, on Friday, August 3, he slept most of the day and woke up at approximately 3:00 p.m. After taking a shower and getting dressed, he left the apartment to do his wash at around 4:00 or 4:30 p.m. at the local laundromat. He did not see Barbara or anyone else outside at that time. After doing his laundry, he left to see a friend, and from there, they both went to Big Jim's Bar in Penndel and stayed until it closed at 2:00 a.m. He didn't remember seeing anyone outside his apartment upon returning home either.

Michael told police he had seen Barbara approximately four or five times, most of the time walking up or down Old Lincoln Highway. Once, he saw her walking up the street with the little girl next door (Kelly). The last time Michael said he saw Barbara was Wednesday, August 1, when she came to his door at approximately 5:30 p.m. and asked if he had a flower. Michael assumed the flower was for Kelly since he had seen them playing together. He had just gotten home and taken off his shoes. He told Barbara he would look to see if he had one. Michael picked up his shoes to bring them into the bedroom when Barbara asked if she could come in. He replied, "Okay," and then continued to the bedroom. Michael assumed she would come in and wait by the front door, but when he placed his shoes on the bedroom floor, he turned around to find Barbara standing right behind him at his bedroom entrance. He then walked into the kitchen, where he had some plants, but he couldn't find any flowers for Barbara, so she left. Michael told investigators that since that incident occurred, he had heard Barbara was a shy girl, but he certainly had not gotten that impression when she so comfortably came into his house that day.

Michael could not remember seeing George or his car parked outside when he left his apartment. However, his roommate, Kevin, was home that evening and reported hearing George talking to someone at around 10:00 p.m. His car was parked there at the time. Michael added that he only really spoke to George and his wife once other than to say hello, and that was when Kevin's car got hit in front of the apartment. There was a note left on Michael's door, and he thought maybe George's wife had put it there, so he went to their door and briefly spoke to him and his wife. It turned out they hadn't put the note there, and he later found out it was Cecelia who had.

Daniel Colacicco, a long-time friend of George and Lori Shaw, lived in Bucks County, Pennsylvania. In an August 22, 1984 interview, Colacicco told detectives he had recently seen George outside his in-laws' home. He stopped to talk to him because George owed him money. George said something unnerving to Colacicco that day, "Giving you a lot of thought about the tape." When detectives asked about the tape George was referring to, Colacicco explained that about four or five months prior, he had worked for a company called M&C Specialties that manufactured special commercial tape.

Colacicco proceeded to a closet and pulled out a black roll of wide, duct-type tape. He had given George several rolls of this type of tape a few months earlier, but in rolls less wide. Colacicco stated he also gave George electrical, Scotch-type, masking, and packaging tape with a string running through it.

Investigators went to M&C Specialties, Colacicco's former employer. They recovered several different types of tape manufactured by this company. Among the types of tape were a roll of two-inch black textured tape and a roll of one-inch clear filament tape, which they collected and secured as evidence. Investigators submitted these items to the FBI Laboratory for comparison with the tape recovered on Barbara's body.

On August 31, investigators executed a search warrant at Shaw's residence. During this search, police found an aquarium filter box with tape on it. Police also found a second box containing tape and secured it as evidence. The tape on the filter box and in the second box appeared to be the same type found on Barbara's body.

All roads led to George Shaw, which made him the primary murder suspect. After Shaw begrudgingly took a polygraph exam, which yielded inconclusive results, detectives lacked the necessary evidence to make an arrest. Despite the connection between the tape found on Barbara's body and the tape found at Shaw's apartment that Colacicco had given him, the forensic technology at the time could not determine if it was indeed the same tape originating from the same source. The district attorney would not approve homicide charges against Shaw based purely on circumstantial evidence. They had no witnesses, no indisputable physical evidence, and no confession despite Koszarek's best efforts. Therefore, Shaw walked out of the police department.

Additionally, in 1984, polygraph tests in Pennsylvania were generally ruled inadmissible. However, rulings on evidence ultimately are held within the discretion of the trial judge, and admissibility varies from state to state, as well as by jurisdiction.

A few weeks later, Shaw and his family moved to neighboring Montgomery County in Upper Moreland, Pennsylvania. The Barbara Rowan case went cold based on the lack of physical evidence or an eyewitness. The fact that Barbara's body was found too late for a rape kit, DNA testing was not available in 1984, and no one followed up on Sanders all served as barriers to an arrest in this case. Barbara's parents, family, and friends were all devastated, and the community was on edge. Local television news stations covered the story, and the hunt continued for Barbara's killer.

Detective Koszarek was promoted to sergeant a few months later and transferred back to the Patrol Division. Detective Rouland remained in the detective division and moved on to new cases.

A couple of months later, in October 1984, the Bensalem PD received an anonymous tip that Sanders was living in West Grove, Pennsylvania as a self-employed landscaper and had been talking about the Rowan homicide.

Later that month, on the same night, *Channel 6 Action News* aired a Crimefighters segment about Barbara's murder at 11:00 p.m. Shortly after that broadcast, an elderly woman was attacked and raped by an intruder in her Upper Moreland, Pennsylvania home (Montgomery County). The rapist had broken into the victim's home through a ground-floor window, assaulted her, bound her with curtain strings, and forcibly raped her. The victim fought the attacker, who eventually fled the scene. The Upper Moreland Police investigated, but no arrests came, and the crime went unsolved for almost a year.

In the spring of 1985, Upper Moreland Police responded to a "peeping Tom" call in the same neighborhood. Upon arrival, officers discovered that the father and brother of the young female victim had confronted the peeper and kept him detained at the scene. The peeper was George Shaw. Upper Moreland Police thoroughly investigated and discovered that the elderly rape victim and the peeping victim lived within a few blocks of each other. Shaw also lived in the neighborhood, and his home was conveniently within walking distance of both victims.

Of course, Shaw denied any allegations of committing either crime. Police then compared fingerprints lifted from the point of entry window of the rape victim's home with Shaw's fingerprints and produced a match. Upper Moreland Police charged Shaw with rape, burglary, and other related offenses. Unfortunately, the case was pled out due to the victim's ill health and the fact that she did not want to participate in a trial. Shaw should have been incarcerated for a long time in state prison, but he got away with a measly year in county jail before being released into the community again.

On two separate occasions, the Upper Moreland PD documented statements that Sanders had talked about Shaw and a murder case in Trevose. In June 1986, Upper

Moreland Police Detective Rick Tidwell interviewed William Wessler. Wessler was friends with twin brothers Bill and Bobby Sanders. At the time of this interview, he had known them for more than ten years.

Wessler cooperated with detectives and admitted that Bobby had called him previously and discussed Barbara's murder. It was clear that Bobby Sanders was holding something back and had been running scared. He told Wessler that his friend, Shaw, had been involved in the girl's murder and that police were looking at him as having some responsibility for it too. Bobby didn't elaborate on how, but said he knew George had killed the girl. Wessler said Bobby was getting extremely paranoid—thinking his phone line was being tapped and that he was being followed and watched everywhere he went. But Bobby had not given any information about what happened or whether he had been involved in the crime.

In another incident, Wessler told detectives that he and Bobby's brother, Bill Sanders, were at a bar one night, and Bill got very drunk. In his inebriated state, Bill told him that Bobby had been involved with Barbara Rowan's murder and George Shaw had killed the girl.

Bill Sanders was arrested in Upper Moreland on March 30, 1998, for public drunkenness. Sergeant Tidwell questioned him about the Barbara Rowan homicide during that time. Bill told police what his brother had confessed to him in 1984—"Bobby was there, and George Shaw date raped the girl, then killed her." Bill was also a drug user and alcoholic. Bill later died due to complications of alcoholism in 2013.

CHAPTER 7
Winding Up

In 2002, I submitted the Barbara Rowan case to the National Center for Missing and Exploited Children, hoping to have it posted on their website for unsolved homicides. I also requested a criminal history check on Shaw. I started a ViCAP (Violent Criminal Apprehension Program) entry booklet for the entire case to be submitted to the New Jersey State Police (NJSP) ViCAP unit, which would then be forwarded to the FBI ViCAP.

ViCAP is an FBI unit that analyzes serial violent and sexual crimes. NJSP ViCAP is the statewide hub for the FBI's ViCAP database. This database is the nation's most comprehensive and extensive information collection on solved and unsolved violent crimes. Law enforcement members nationwide can obtain access to this database to enter and analyze their individual cases. Intending to link similar cases and help solve them, the FBI ViCAP collects information regarding various types of crimes—whether or not the offender has been arrested or identified—including homicides, sexual assaults, abductions, missing persons where foul play is suspected, and unidentified human remains, where the manner of death is known or suspected to be a homicide.

I placed requests with the Pennsylvania Department of Transportation to obtain photographs from Shaw, Bobby Sanders, Wessler, and Colacicco's driver's licenses.

In search of possible latent fingerprints or fibers, Detective Vandergrift and I examined the tape found on Barbara's body with a Crimescope but found nothing. A Crimescope uses ultraviolet imaging to locate invisible fingerprints without using powders, fumes, or any chemicals that can be destructive to evidence.

Next, we prepared several items collected at the crime scene in 1984 to re-submit evidence for forensic testing, and they were sent to the FBI Laboratory. A list of persons to be re-interviewed included Lori Shaw, Wiliam Wessler, Bobby Sanders, Bill Sanders, Cecelia Biggs, Hayes Biggs, Joe Snow, Lois Warden, and numerous others.

I contacted Dave Rouland and asked if we could meet to discuss the Rowan case over coffee. He was happy to help however he could, and we met at the Club House Diner, a very familiar place to Bensalem cops. He told me about the case and how things had played out over a couple of sandwiches, a pot of coffee, and a half-pack of cigarettes (Rouland was a heavy smoker). Bill Koszarek had insisted on performing their last interview with Shaw, which resulted in an unpleasant and unproductive outcome. Shaw knew they couldn't hold him and asked if he was being charged. Rouland and Koszarek could not legally keep him there, so he got up and walked out.

"It was the one case that has always haunted me because it was absolutely a solvable case and was never solved," Rouland revealed. It seemed evident that Bobby Sanders knew the truth and was lying to detectives. He had a strong history of getting drunk and running his mouth. Rouland had no doubt that the case was solvable and believed that Bobby Sanders was "the key" to solving it.

In the fall of 2003, I sent letters to Bobby Sanders and William Wessler, requesting to speak with them about an "ongoing investigation." We first heard from Wessler, who was apprehensive and seemed irritated after a bout of phone tag with us. "I'm not gonna play any games," Wessler asserted. He insisted that we tell him why we wanted to talk to him if we wanted him to cooperate.

An interview with Luther Sanders, father of Bobby, took place later that month after he had signed for the certified letter mailed to Bobby. Luther called detectives regarding the letter and stated his son was in Montgomery County Prison awaiting trial, scheduled for some time in January. He gave us Bobby's prison inmate number and the Montgomery County Correctional Facility phone number. Seemingly, Bobby was in custody at the facility for charges from Upper Moreland Township for driving under the influence, fleeing and eluding police, and state parole violations. Next, I sent the tape recovered from Barbara's body to the Pennsylvania State Police in Bethlehem, along with a sample of her hair and hairbrush to be examined for any DNA profiles other than her own. That following March, the DNA analysis report established that no other DNA profiles were identified from the items submitted.

In the spring of 2004, while attending a class at the Bucks County Police Training Center, I ran into Detective Mike Mosiniak, who was attending the same training class. Mike and I had met in the summer of 1989 in North Wildwood, New Jersey. We had a mutual friend named Tom and, one weekend, Tom and Moz came over to my grandmother's house in North Wildwood and crashed there after a night of drinking at Moore's Inlet in nearby Anglesea. At the time, Mosiniak had just been hired by the Warminster Police Department. We hit it off well.

A few years later, Mosiniak left his job as a Warminster Police sergeant for a position as county detective with the Bucks County District Attorney's Office. We hadn't stayed in touch. But now, after some small talk and catching up, the conversation changed to work, and I mentioned reopening the Barbara Rowan case. Unlike everyone else I worked with at the time, Mosiniak showed a genuine interest in the case. I knew then that he would be a great partner to team up with.

I certainly had my fill of naysayers. One of the senior detectives overheard me talking about the case one day and, in a very smug and sarcastic manner, said, "I know who killed Barbara Rowan—George Shaw did." Then he laughed. I snapped back at him, "Well then, why don't you arrest him?!" Now with a stupid look on his face, his response was, "Well, the DA said there wasn't enough evidence." This idiot didn't know evidence from a hole in the ground, and I found him to be plain fucking lazy. If an investigation took him out of his comfort zone (his desk or the coffee pot), it didn't get worked on, let alone solved. To borrow a quote from my old friend, Don Kueny, "He couldn't find an elephant in a phone booth!"

There were many other naysayer moments along the way, and I found myself adopting the cutthroat Ray Liotta attitude from the movie *Goodfellas*. Is the case too old? Fuck you; I'm solving it. Evidence is circumstantial. Fuck you; I'm solving it. Witnesses won't be honest. Fuck you; I'm solving it. I refused to back down from this case, no matter what anyone said or did to discourage me. The case needed to be solved.

I realized I had to be more assertive, especially in police work, or I would get eaten alive by both criminals and fellow cops, but primarily by cops. As a uniform patrolman, I would have interactions and conflicts with criminals, but they were usually over quickly. I wouldn't have to see the defendant again until court, and I rarely interviewed them. On the other hand, as a detective, hours of interviewing suspects is a routine part of the job, and it can be mentally draining and emotionally challenging. That shy young boy in me had to take the back seat if I was going to be effective.

On April 6, 2004, Detectives Jen Cannon, Mike Mosiniak, and I met with Montgomery County Detective

Sam Gallen at the Montgomery County DA's Office in Norristown, Pennsylvania. At our request, Gallen brought Bobby Sanders into his office from Montgomery County Prison so we could interview him. Sanders' account of August 3, 1984, was that Shaw had contacted him by phone and said he had meth. Shaw picked up Sanders at his house in Upper Moreland Township, and they drove to Shaw's apartment on Old Lincoln Highway in the Trevose section of Bensalem. It was dark outside then, and they parked in the rear of Shaw's residence. They entered the apartment, and Sanders claimed he did not see anyone there.

Shaw went into his bedroom and closed the door at that time. Bobby believed Shaw was shooting meth. He stayed in the bedroom for approximately thirty minutes. When Shaw finally exited the bedroom, "he was covered in sweat, hyped up, edgy, and jumpy," described Sanders. Shaw told him he had to go around back and move his car to the front of the building, then walked out of the apartment. Sanders walked into the bedroom and found it in complete disarray. The bed sheets were rolled up in a ball, and "it looked like a tornado went through it," Sanders claimed. Sanders also noticed that the bedroom window was at ground level.

Shaw returned to the apartment about five minutes later and said he had to go elsewhere. Sanders mentioned that while Shaw was gone, he heard someone banging on the front door and answered it. An agitated man was at the door (Robert Rowan). He was upset and demanded to know where his daughter was. Sanders told him he didn't know and that there wasn't anyone else inside the apartment besides him and Shaw. Sanders didn't think the man believed him because he said he was going to call the police before he walked away.

According to Sanders, he did not tell Shaw about this after he returned to the apartment the second time. Shaw never said where he had gone, and they only stayed at the apartment for a little while longer before he drove Sanders back to his father's house.

Sanders was angry with Shaw for all the aggravation he had caused him because of that night and stayed away from him afterward. When asked what he meant by "aggravation," Sanders explained he had been questioned by the police on multiple occasions. He mentioned several times that he had thought about this incident a lot over the years and felt terrible because of what happened to the girl.

Sanders didn't see Shaw for a while after the day Barbara went missing. But when he finally did run into him, he told Shaw to stay away from him. He never gave Shaw an explanation why, and Shaw never asked him, but he felt that Shaw already knew the reason. Sanders admitted he just wanted to get high that night and said he got "dragged into this."

Further along in the interview with Sanders, he told detectives that Shaw was in the bedroom with the door closed when he heard "rustling sounds" coming from the bedroom. "Shaw could have had the girl dead or alive in the bedroom when he was in there and put her outside through the bedroom window before putting the body into his car," stated Sanders. This would be when Shaw went outside and said he was moving his car from the rear to the front of the building. But Sanders said he didn't know for sure what had actually occurred. Sanders was trying to hint at what happened without outright saying it. We wanted him to come clean, but he wouldn't talk anymore. He just stared at us like a deer in headlights.

In a statement Sanders had given to police in 1984, he mentioned Shaw's daughter Kelly being present at the apartment and even told detectives that Shaw had bathed her. Now he was claiming that Kelly was, in fact, not present in the apartment and that when he used the bathroom (which he believed was the only bathroom in the apartment), he noticed that the bathtub was filled with dirty dishes and pots and pans, so it would have been impossible to use the bathtub.

We called Sanders out on being deceptive and withholding information. This made him nervous. He said he wanted to tell the truth but needed to talk to his girlfriend first. When asked why he needed to speak to her first, he kept repeating that he needed to talk to her and offered no other reason. He then refused to communicate with us, and the interview ended.

Phone records at the prison reflected the outgoing phone calls Sanders had placed to his girlfriend, Donna Zabroski; his father, Luther; and his brother, Bill. These calls were taped and preserved under the Montgomery

County Correctional Facility policy. We obtained a copy of the recorded telephone calls made by Sanders in prison to aid the investigation further.

Sanders' first outgoing telephone call following our visit with him was to Zabroski. On the recording, Zabroski asks Sanders if there had been "anything new on what he told her about." Sanders responded, "I gotta call them up; only Me, the Lord, and the guy who did it know what happened."

He made a second call to his brother. "That George Shaw stuff was brought up again," Bobby said. Then he asked his brother what he had told the cops before and referred to Wessy talking to the cops. "Wessy" is William Wessler.

Bobby then called his father. "Just because I was there doesn't mean I saw anything. I didn't see him do it," Bobby declared. This statement just indicated that Bobby was in denial about what happened.

Further along, in April 2004, the tape found on Barbara's body was taken to the FBI Laboratory in Quantico, Virginia, along with the rolls of tape recovered in Shaw's apartment back in 1984, for comparison. The FBI receives cases regularly from all over the country. Due to the tremendous backlog, it took close to seven years for the analysis to be completed, so we waited.

CHAPTER 8
Nan: Her Way

My grandmother was born Anne M. Manning on October 6, 1923, but I called her "Nan." She was one of my most vital and influential role models. Nan was one of eight children and became a war bride when she married William Hawkins of New York during World War II. William was a submariner in the U.S. Navy and a crewman on the *USS Bullhead* SS 332 Balao class submarine. The Bullhead had only three war patrols before she was listed as "Overdue and Presumed Lost" on August 6, 1945. Her last known location was somewhere in the Java Sea. William, my grandfather, never returned home. While he was at sea, Anne gave birth to their daughter, Joyce Anne Hawkins, my mother. Sadly, my mother and her father never met.

At the time, a man by the name of Martin Sheridan was the only war correspondent allowed on a U.S. submarine in wartime. He wrote a book about his collective experiences aboard the *USS Bullhead* titled

Overdue and Presumed Lost: The Story of the USS Bullhead, first published in 1947. Sheridan was on the vessel during the first two war patrols, but not the third, which was the last time the submarine was seen. The *USS Bullhead* was the last U.S. Navy vessel sunk by enemy action during WWII. It was likely to have occurred the same day the atomic bomb was dropped on Hiroshima.

To this day, my mother is terrified of the ocean. I remember as a kid, my father once had a twenty-five-foot boat. He made my mom feel bad about not going on trips and pressured her into going on the boat. She would get the most violent panic attacks I'd ever seen, and we'd have to turn around and return to land. I never made the connection until recently, but it finally dawned on me that she feared the water because her father died at sea. My mother loves the beach but will never get into the ocean.

On October 23, 1948, Anne got married again. This time, to Joseph "Buddy" Manning of Manhattan, New York, who quickly adopted my mother as his child. They resided in the Riverdale section of the Bronx on Palisade Avenue, overlooking the Hudson River. Buddy had graduated from NYU and worked as an accountant in New York City. He and Anne also owned and operated Gorman's Bar in the Chelsea section of Manhattan. Sadly, Buddy succumbed to bone cancer and passed away on January 26, 1967. He was only forty-seven years old. That was strike two for me in the grandfather department.

Buddy's brother Mike, or "Mickey," filled his shoes well when it came to having a grandfatherly type of person around. When I was a kid, he would take me to the boardwalk to play air hockey and used to torture me over New York teams beating Philly teams. It was comforting to feel as though I got to know a little of Buddy through Uncle Mickey. He was the best and he was also a war hero like William Hawkins. My Aunt Flo, Mickey's wife, loved to cook and made great Italian food! I miss them a lot.

Uncle Bucky was Nan's brother and also a WWII vet. He was injured in the war and became a paraplegic. Everyone should have an Uncle Bucky. If you don't have an Uncle Bucky, you should get one. He died on Christmas Eve of 1980, but I had a chance to spend time with him until I was almost eleven years old. He used to sit and talk with me and tell me important things like how bartenders comb their hair and if you want to get to know someone, you have to have a drink with them. Sometimes he would send me to his room for his "medicine." He would say, "come here." When I approached him, he'd slip me a few bucks and say, "Go get my medicine for me." This was code for "get the whiskey." I would go into his room, find his bottle of whiskey, and bring it to him.

Bucky and I used to watch baseball games together all the time. It amazed me how sharp he was. We would watch the Phillies, and he knew every player, their position, and their batting average. The year he died, 1980, the Phillies won the World Series.

My dad and I went to Game Six of that series on October 21, 1980, at Veterans Stadium in South Philly. The Phillies beat the Kansas City Royals 4-1 after Tug

McGraw struck out Willie Wilson for the third out in the top of the 9th inning. I will never forget that night. It was fantastic! Tug McGraw, the father of famed country singer Tim McGraw, was my favorite player because he was charismatic. I even named my dog after him. He's a Pomapoo named Tug, and he rules. Around 2001, I met Tug and Tim McGraw when country radio station 92.5 WXTU sponsored a big country concert at Philadelphia Park Racetrack in Bensalem. I still have a picture of me with Tim and Tug McGraw. It was exciting to meet my childhood hero!

On May 7, 1987, Nan's great-granddaughter, my daughter Caitlin Marie McMullin, was born. Nan treated me like gold, but Caitlin, she was more like triple platinum! The day we brought Caitlin home from the hospital, a lovely picture was taken of me holding Caitlin up as I was about to kiss her. Nan had it enlarged and framed and kept it on her bedroom dresser.

Although Nan's family was small, she ran it like the Marine Corps. Caitlin's early arrival in my life was perfect timing since she had Nan for over twenty years. Nan had another little girl to dress up, buy things for, and teach to be, shall we say, assertive. As I said, Nan was always a straight shooter—she told it like it was and did things her way. Just like Father Kilty, you always knew where she stood.

Nan battled cancer three times in her life, from the early 1970s, when she survived a lung removal, until it finally claimed her on October 16, 2007. She was bedridden for two weeks before she died and dropped her Claddagh ring on the floor. For those of you who may be unfamiliar, a Claddagh ring is a traditional Irish ring. The hands represent friendship, the heart represents love, and the crown represents loyalty. It had rolled underneath the bed, so she asked me to pick it up. But because I was busy caring for her, the request went in one ear and out the other, and I never retrieved it from underneath the bed. I will get back to that story in a bit.

Nan also loved listening to Frank Sinatra. When she was eventually placed in hospice care and became unresponsive, I would come home from work, play Sinatra, and talk to her. Caitlin was in nursing school then and learned more in those last two weeks about being a nurse than in two and a half years of nursing school. She took such good care of her grandmother and made everyone very proud. Back in 1976, Nan took me to a Sinatra show at the Valley Forge Music Center. To this day, I cannot hear a Sinatra song—especially *My Way*—without thinking of her.

On the night Nan took her last breath, I sat on one side of the bed while Caitlin sat opposite me. We hugged each other and cried as Nan lay peacefully between us. I looked down at the foot of the bed and saw the reflection of all three of us in the dresser mirror. I couldn't help but notice the framed photograph on Nan's dresser of a seventeen-year-old me holding up brand new baby Caitlin while kissing her.

Knowing that Nan, Caitlin, and I were all together at the start of Caitlin's life and now together at the end

Nan, Chris, and Caitlin

of Nan's life became a very surreal moment for me as I witnessed things come full circle.

After the undertaker came and removed her body, I didn't know what to do with my emotions and became very angry. I found myself stripping the sheets off her bed and picking up the mattress to put out for the trash. She had previously told me that, after she died, I was to throw out her bed because nobody wants a bed that someone died in. I stepped over the bed frame to begin taking it apart and felt a sudden, piercing pain as I put my foot on the floor. I picked my foot up and found Nan's Claddagh ring with a small drop of blood where the ring's crown had pierced through the skin. I am sure that was her way of telling me, "I told you to pick it up two weeks ago, ya horse's ass; next time, don't procrastinate!" Whenever I

17-year-old Chris and infant daughter, Caitlin
Credit: Chris McMullin

find myself procrastinating, I remember this moment and move forward.

Anne was returned to New York and laid to rest with Buddy. I miss her.

CHAPTER 9
Moving Forward

On April 7, 2004, Detective Mosiniak and I met with Kimberly Sullivan for a re-interview. She was part of the crew that hung out at the McDonald's in Hatboro and recalled the events on August 3, 1984, involving Shaw and Bobby Sanders. Sullivan stated that on August 3, 1984, she was at the McDonald's restaurant in Hatboro Borough with her then-boyfriend, Mark Litman. Sometime between 7:45 and 8:00 p.m., she observed Shaw drive onto Monument Avenue adjacent to the McDonald's. Shaw stopped and spoke to another individual named Robert Romanski, then came over and got Sanders. They walked back to Shaw's car, at which time Sanders walked over to Sullivan and asked to borrow her "points" (needles for injecting methamphetamine). She handed them over to Sanders, and he said he was going for a ride with Shaw to see his new house in Trevose.

Five hours later, at approximately 1:00 a.m., Sullivan was at the Mobil gas station located at York Road and

County Line Road in Hatboro Borough. She observed Shaw drive past but stated Sanders was not with him inside the vehicle. Thirty minutes later, around 1:30 a.m., she was still at the gas station and observed Sanders hitchhiking in that area. He returned her "points" to her at that time.

Detective Mosiniak conducted a separate interview with Robert Romanski on April 8, 2004. Romanski stated he used to live with a guy named Gary Burros. He recalled being at the McDonald's in Hatboro Borough on August 3, 1984, when he observed Shaw drive up to that location at dusk. He believed it was between 8:00 and 9:00 p.m. Shaw was alone in his vehicle when he arrived, but Sanders and Shaw left together to shoot meth at Shaw's apartment.

Romanski did not go with them but remembered Shaw returning to the Mobil gas station in Hatboro Borough at approximately 1:00 a.m. He was alone in the car and acting very nervous and "not himself," according to Romanski. Shaw asked them if they knew where Sanders was, but they didn't. Around 1:30 a.m., Romanski saw Sanders hitchhiking and said he was "out of sorts." After that night, Shaw's Pontiac LeMans disappeared, and he told Romanski he'd had to get the car towed. Burros had reportedly seen Shaw's car at a junkyard.

The word on the street back in 1984 was that Shaw had killed Barbara and Sanders was also involved, according to Romanski. He believed Sanders knew of this and was really scared. He stopped coming around after that night. But before finding out about the murder, Sanders cautioned,

"George Shaw is bad news." He described Shaw as scary and said he was "big and mean when high on drugs."

Romanski claimed that Shaw liked his wife working nights because it made it easy for him to get high. "He would go out at night while his wife was at work and sometimes would have his daughter Kelly in the car with him. But Shaw's parents often watched Kelly for him," explained Romanski.

There was talk on the street of Shaw killing the girl over a bad drug deal. According to Romanski, at the time, there was a guy named Tom who was a big drug dealer. "After we knew about the murder, Dan Colacicco came to see me one day. He used to drive a pickup truck. He asked me to help him move something heavy from the back of it. When we went to the back of the truck, he attacked me and tied me up with duct tape and rope. Basically, he hog-tied me," told Romanski. "I started to yell for help, and he would hit me and tell me to shut up. He left me in the back of the truck and drove to Gary's apartment. After I yelled again, he untied me, and I ran away." He continued, "Dan Colacicco and George Shaw were tight with each other. I think I was tied up because they wanted to scare me."

On April 15, 2004, Mark Litman was interviewed by Detective Mosiniak and stated that, in August 1984, he had been dating Kimberly Sullivan on and off for approximately three years. Litman said he remembered Shaw and said he drove a big Impala. Litman bought methamphetamine from Shaw three times. He recalled that the night at the McDonald's in Hatboro was the third time. Litman had gotten paid that night and asked Shaw for some methamphetamine. After he gave him money for an "eight ball" (an eighth of an ounce/3 to 3.5 grams), Shaw left to get it. Litman thought he got ripped off because Shaw didn't return until much later that night. They met up at the gas station in Hatboro. He recalled the methamphetamine Shaw did eventually give him "was shit." He described Shaw as "very nervous and sweaty" when he returned but stated Shaw got like that when he was high. Litman believed this was the last time he ever spoke to him.

He remembered seeing Sanders that night but couldn't recall if he had gotten into Shaw's car when he (Shaw) left the McDonald's. He also didn't recall if Sanders was with Shaw when Shaw returned with the methamphetamine, and he didn't remember seeing Sanders hitchhiking. Litman said that Sullivan carried "works" with her then. He said she would lend them out to people in return for methamphetamine.

The following month, I spoke to Robert Hazard at his home. I reminded him of the report he gave to detectives on August 17, 1984, regarding a pair of blue shorts and underwear he had found near where Barbara Rowan's body had been discovered. Hazard led me to where he had found the shorts but didn't recall seeing underwear with them, although he had reported that in his original statement in 1984. He remembered that the shorts were larger, perhaps an adult male size, but he could not recall if the police had taken the shorts into evidence.

CHAPTER 10
On Set

Here is an interesting story from my childhood. When I was six, my dad took me to my first Phillies game at Veterans Stadium. The Phillies were playing the Atlanta Braves. I had seen many games on television with my dad, but this was a new experience. Right on the field in front of us were legendary players Mike Schmidt, Greg Luzinski, Larry Bowa, Steve Carlton, and Tug McGraw. As I mentioned, McGraw was always my favorite pitcher, and his performance in the 1980 World Series would seal that deal a few years later. His charisma and energy were unrivaled. The home run-hitting power of Schmidt and Luzinski was incredible, and the speed of Bowa was remarkable. As for Carlton, he was just calm and composed all the time.

At the top of one of the early innings, a foul ball found its way to the right side of the field, where we were sitting. Everyone stood up to try to catch it, naively including me, and I got slammed right in between the eyes by the ball. Surprisingly, it hurt like hell but didn't knock me out. This was early evidence of how hard-headed I am. I remember my dad picking me up and carrying me up the steps to find help. A uniformed police officer met us and took me from my dad as we headed into the medic station. One minute I was looking up at a foul ball; the next minute, a cop was carrying me to a first aid station. In the plus column, I got to go into the locker room and meet several Phillies players while nursing my head with a bag of ice. It was well worth it. Unfortunately, the Braves won the game that day. But I got to keep the ball that whacked me out, and I still have it. (insert photo if wanted)

This leads me to another interesting story from my childhood. When I was about five or six, I remember telling my mom I wanted to be on television. She said if I wanted to do that, I would have to go far away to Hollywood, California, because that's where TV shows and movies were made. One would think that a woman born and raised in the Bronx would have realized how huge of a domain NYC was (and still is) for film production. That could have been her way of keeping me close to home.

A few years later, I saw the original *Rocky* movie. When Sylvester Stallone ran up the art museum steps, I recognized the building from a recent class trip I had gone on for school. At that moment, I thought, "Rocky was not made in California. It was made right here in Philly." Fast forward a few years later to *Rocky III* (1983). Stallone cast the Abraham Lincoln High School marching band in the film. The robe Rocky Balboa (Stallone) wore in *Rocky II* was black and gold, representing Lincoln's school colors. I learned from my lifelong friend Fred Eyrich (who was in the Lincoln H.S. marching band) that Stallone went to Lincoln and was from our area. Stallone was from Holme Circle—next to Lexington Park, not California. Lincoln's marching band was used in the scene at the Philadelphia Art Museum when they unveiled the Rocky statue right before Clubber Lang started running his mouth at him. Hearing this inspired me. If Stallone was from our area and could be an actor, I could too. Even though I am not well-known in the acting world, I still credit Stallone for the inspiration and continue to work at it.

In 1998, I got my start in acting. The Bucks County DA's office, in partnership with the Network of Victim Assistance (NOVA), was producing training videos on "How to Testify in Court Properly" and "How to Investigate Domestic Violence Properly." Fred Harran, the deputy director of public safety, told me that a production company was hired to bring in actors, along with director Peter Halperin, but they also wanted some real cops to participate in the project. Greg Young and I were cast as cops. Undeniably, this was typecasting, but we were okay with it. Instead of going to work, we went to the production set for the next three days. The "acting bug" bit me after this, and I began taking acting classes and submitting for roles through casting agencies.

In 2003, I joined the Screen Actors Guild (SAG), which opened more doors in the acting world. SAG, now known as SAG-AFTRA, is an American labor union that represents over 100,000 film and television principals and background performers worldwide. Its mission is to establish and enforce appropriate compensation rates, benefits, and working conditions for its performers.

Over the years, I got some background work on the television show *Hack*, in which I frequently played the role of a detective in the background—hard to believe, I know. I was fortunate to have background roles in a few Hollywood motion pictures, including *Jersey Girl* and *National Treasure*, which also helped me earn my SAG card.

Fast forward to 2010. I was talking to a friend named David Roehm Sr., a U.S. Navy vet from WWII and a nice guy. I told him about my grandfather, whom I'd never met because he and the rest of the *USS Bullhead* crew were declared "overdue and presumed lost." David did a lot of acting in the Philadelphia area, and that's how I had the privilege of knowing him. He was a good man and a good friend. David mentioned that the Heery Casting Agency was casting a cop role in *The Dark Fields*, set to film in Philadelphia. The name was later changed to *Limitless* and starred such A-list actors as Robert De Niro and Pennsylvania native Bradley Cooper. I immediately jumped on Heery's website and reviewed the breakdown for the role. I submitted for it right away and expected the usual no-call. Surprisingly, I got a call for an audition the following week.

I went to Heery's office in Old City, picked up the sides and scene breakdown, and filmed my audition. In short, the scene was a uniformed cop (myself) coming into an apartment where a murder had just been reported. He encounters Eddie Morra, the character played by Bradley Cooper. When my character enters the apartment and sees Morra, he yells, "Let me see your hands!" It would be a significant role since it was a big-budget film with a SAG contract, not to mention a speaking scene with the lead actor.

I got a callback, and this time I auditioned in full uniform because I heard the director, Neil Burger, would be present. The next thing I knew, Diane Heery called and told me I was booked for the role. At that point, I sought an agent and landed with the Reinhard Agency.

I showed up in Old City, Philadelphia, for my shoot and was given a small trailer to get dressed in. Years of working background had finally paid off, and this was a huge bump up. After going through makeup and wardrobe, I was brought to the film set at a nearby condominium building. That is where I met Bradley Cooper for the first time. He came right over to me and said hello. He was a nice guy, down to earth. We exchanged introductions, and I told him we had a mutual friend. Cooper is from Abington and attended high school with one of my co-workers from the Bensalem PD, Larry Leith. Larry asked me to give Cooper one of his business cards, which I did. They have since reconnected.

We began blocking out and rehearsing the scene with Neil Burger several times. But when we filmed, Cooper wanted me to go hands-on and push him back into the wall. He was great to work with and said, "On the day, make sure you don't hold back."

"On the day" was Cooper's expression for when we filmed the scene. So that's exactly what I did, and we got the scene done in about three takes. It was definitely a great experience that I will always be thankful for.

I joke that Cooper "stole" my role in the well-known film *Wedding Crashers*. In 2004 or early 2005, I got an audition at Pat Moran Casting in Baltimore, Maryland. There, I read for the part of Sack Lodge. I remember reading the lines and pretending to talk on the phone with a character named Trapster. I didn't book this role because Bradley Cooper did! I remember watching the scene in the movie and thinking, "No wonder I didn't book it! He played it completely differently!"

Ten years went by after my role on *Limitless*. During this time, I auditioned for dozens of parts without success. I knew M. Knight Shyamalan had a project filming in Philly, initially called *Crumpet*. I had auditioned for it the previous year but didn't book it. My confidence was in the gutter, and I questioned whether I would continue to audition. Then my agent called again and sent me to another audition for the same project, now called *Servant*.

Servant was a psychological thriller television series on Apple TV. It stars Lauren Ambrose and Toby Kebbell. Lauren Ambrose is well-known for the HBO series *Six Feet Under*, in which she played the role of Claire Fisher. Toby Kebbell is known for his roles in films such as *Fantastic Four* and *Warcraft*. The part I auditioned for was that of a patrol officer, and I booked it! I got to shoot my scenes with Ambrose. I was nervous because I had to work with a green screen and act like I was watching a TV news broadcast while she was talking to me. I had never done a scene like that, and

Ambrose picked up on it. She was very down-to-earth and coached me. She helped me immensely on that set, and I am thankful to her. We pulled the scene together nicely. After three days of filming on *Servant*, I had another principal role in the books.

Since then, I have played a role on the television series *Law & Order SVU* as an FDNY captain. We filmed in February 2021, and it aired a couple of months later in April. The title was "Welcome to the Pedo Motel," episode 10 of Season 22.

CHAPTER 11
Christian Rojas

In 2005, during the center of my consumption in the Rowan case, I was young, just in my early thirties, but those were the days when I could wake up in the morning and start the day without my entire body hurting for no good reason. Then, around the same time, I was faced with another horrendous homicide.

Heather Lavelle is one of those people who holds a *special* place in my heart—which to me means there's a special place in hell for people like her. Lavelle was the first female in Bucks County to face the death penalty. She didn't get a death sentence because Christian Rojas' family members were faithful Christians and didn't believe in punishment by death. I remember them telling the judge this during their victim impact statement. I think the court honored their wishes. On August 27, 2005, Christian's close friend James Lawrence found him dead in a tub full of dark, bloody water inside his Bensalem apartment. A pillow covered Christian's face, and his hands and feet were bound with electrical wire. His killer, or killers, had stuffed socks inside his mouth and tied another pair around his neck like a makeshift noose. He was fully clothed and wet.

Christian was supposed to pick James up from the airport that night, and when he didn't show up or answer his phone, James called for a ride from another friend, who dropped him off at Christian's apartment. He entered the apartment through an unlocked patio door.

It looked like hell had broken loose inside the apartment. A three-part sectional couch had all its cushions slashed with a knife. The stuffing was everywhere, but no blood was on the couch. A framed 8 x 10 photograph knocked down from a living room wall had been shattered onto the floor. The photo included Christian, a young woman, and another man beside her. At the time, I thought this meant something significant and believed the killer(s) had intentionally smashed it out of anger. The attacker(s) had ripped curtains and dumped drawers on the floor. Whoever had been there went out of their way to ransack the place.

An oversized, stuffed Tasmanian devil had been slashed open, like one of those prizes from a boardwalk game. The stuffing consisted of those little Styrofoam beads, and the entire apartment was covered with them. I've seen my fair share of crime scenes, but this one was extreme. Not just because Christian was found in a bathtub full of bloody water but because blood was spattered on nearly every wall, especially the hallway. Christian's last few hours on this earth were nothing short of torture.

Strangely, several unopened condoms were floating in the bathtub water. I could tell Christian had been forced into the tub against his will. Higher up along the shower tiles of the tub were bloodstains that appeared to have been made by his face and head because some hair was mixed in with the blood. It was evident that his head had been smashed into the wall while he was on his feet in the tub. There were several lacerations on Christian's scalp, measuring one-half to one inch long. The murderer had taken wire splicers from a tool kit in the apartment and made minor cuts to his scalp to torture him. There was obvious trauma to Christian's head, but the final cause of death was uncertain. It appeared that the person who did this knew Christian and was very angry with him.

The following day, an unidentified man showed up at the police department, wanting to speak to officers about Christian. When I walked out to the lobby to meet him, I recognized the mysterious man's face from the smashed photograph in the apartment. He introduced himself as John DeMarco. He lived in Bensalem and worked with Christian. He had met Christian in Costa Rica and recruited him to the United States to work for their company as a web designer in 2003. Christian had temporarily lived with DeMarco and his wife in the U.S. until he got settled on his own (the smashed photo was of the three of them). DeMarco had heard about Christian's death through James Lawrence's family and wanted to provide some information to the police. He revealed that Christian was preparing to leave the company, but not on bad terms. The business owners could not give Christian more money, so he had taken another job elsewhere.

DeMarco gave us some insight into Christian's past relationship with a girl named Heather. He said she was an attractive blonde in her thirties who stood around six feet tall. Heather and Christian had dated for three months and lived together in Christian's apartment for a little while, but Christian kicked her out when he discovered she was using drugs. However, DeMarco didn't know her last name, and we needed a last name to learn more about her.

According to the autopsy, Christian had died approximately thirty-six hours before the discovery of his body. No eyewitnesses saw anyone going in or out of the apartment. The killer or killers got quite the head start. The medical examiner determined the cause of death to be blunt force trauma from approximately fifteen blows to the head with a dull instrument. Christian did not believe in keeping his money in the bank and had held his cash at home. But no significant amounts of money, nor a safe, were ever found inside the apartment.

Some of Christian's friends came forward with concerns about the people Christian worked for, the Lumberto brothers. He'd had nasty arguments with them and expressed concerns about his employment there. Allegedly, there was a connection between the brothers and organized crime. The Lumbertos had even asked me if I knew Frank Friel because he had investigated and arrested associates of theirs in the past.

Upon interviewing the brothers, they expressed that they were aware of Christian's plans to leave the company but had no ill feelings toward him. They were both very cooperative and admitted to loaning Christian money to help pay his rent and bills, but they weren't upset about the money he owed them. I never got any indication of bad blood between Christian and the brothers. Maybe things hadn't worked out perfectly between them, but they appeared genuinely upset about Christian's death and were trying to help us get to the bottom of it.

James Lawrence finally remembered Heather's last name and notified the police. Her name was Heather Lavelle. After doing a background check on Lavelle through our database and checking with some adjoining jurisdictions, I found other incidents she had been involved in, including some reports about disputes with her current boyfriend, James Savage. Savage and Lavelle had been fighting with each other just three weeks before Christian's death. Lavelle had filed a report alleging physical abuse. The subsequent investigation also revealed that Savage was previously married and had since been widowed. But before his wife's passing, she had filed a report and pressed charges against him for threatening her with a rifle. This raised significant red flags. The name "Savage" seemed appropriate for him, if he had done this level of violence. He was six feet, four inches tall and weighed 260 pounds.

Matt Coughlin was a local newspaper reporter for the *Bucks County Times*, and he put out a story a few days after the murder. Christian had arranged to stay with a friend in St. Louis, where he planned to relocate for his new job. As fate would have it, this friend saw Matt's newspaper article online and contacted him with some insightful news about Christian's life. Christian provided valuable details about his tumultuous relationship with Heather Lavelle and her addiction problems. Coughlin forwarded the information to me.

Christian drove a green 1998 Saturn company car, which was not in its usual parking spot and nowhere to be found in the apartment complex. We visited the address where Savage and Lavelle had had the reported dispute three weeks prior. We weren't sure what to expect. Savage's mother, Jackie, answered the door. It turned out that Savage's eight-year-old daughter and his mother lived there. Mrs. Savage verified that James and Lavelle were, in fact, in a relationship and had been staying there. She didn't like Lavelle and had kicked her out a few days earlier, although she wouldn't specify why. Jackie said that Lavelle had packed her stuff, and James had taken his mother's car to move her out. But that was short-lived—they both showed up in a small, green vehicle at Jackie's workplace the next day. They transferred Lavelle's belongings from Jackie's car to the mysterious green vehicle, claiming they were going to the shore for the week. The green car described sounded like the car Christian drove.

We (Bensalem Police and Bucks County detectives) didn't know exactly where Savage and Lavelle were heading, but we searched high and low for the stolen Saturn at local hotels. We finally caught a break and found the hotel they had stayed in. We recovered the room registration and video surveillance footage of Lavelle and Savage walking the hallways, exiting the hotel, and driving away in a green Saturn. But we still needed to find out where they were going.

Now that they were the primary suspects in the murder, we obtained a warrant for their arrest in connection with the stolen car and entered them and the green vehicle and its license plate as wanted into NCIC. On September 1, 2005, there was a high-speed chase between the occupants of the green Saturn and police in Nags Head, North Carolina. It was a complete, blown-out pursuit. The chase continued for several minutes after the suspects refused to pull over for a traffic violation. When the police ran the plate, they learned the car was stolen and the occupants were murder suspects, so they continued the pursuit. Eventually, the police dropped stop sticks along the highway to disable the vehicle and end the chase.

The suspects exited the vehicle and fled on foot toward the beach. Both were caught and arrested. Lavelle, now a brunette, and a newly red-haired Savage had attempted to conceal their identities by changing their hair color but had forgotten to ditch their driver's licenses, so they were both easily identified. I went to Nags Head with two other detectives from the DA's office. We obtained a warrant to search the car, which was now impounded. We opened the trunk, and in there, we found what we believed to be the murder weapon, a pair of blood-stained brass knuckles.

We interviewed Savage first at the Dare County Prison. He was a large, menacing individual, and I knew that if he decided to get angry, we wouldn't stand a chance against him. At first, he tried to play the tough guy but surprisingly remained calm throughout the interview. After being Mirandized, the initial story Savage gave was that he and Lavelle had gone to Christian's apartment and intercepted a robbery in progress by three Puerto Rican males. We let him continue with this story for thirty minutes. When we asked Savage how he obtained a cut we observed on his hand, he claimed the robbers had inflicted the wound during their altercation. Now was the time to change tactics with Savage, and for purposes of persuasion, we began to ask questions directing the blame on Christian. We asked questions that suggested Christian had provoked his own murder, such as, "Did Christian do something to cause you to get into a fight over Heather?" This tactic worked, and Savage spoke with us and ultimately told us what happened and followed that up with a signed confession. There was a jealousy factor in his attack on Christian because Lavelle made up a story that Christian had tried to have sex with her. She claimed Christian was unaware she still had a key to his apartment. While he was at work, Lavelle and Savage entered the apartment and waited for Christian to return home. Savage confessed to throwing the condoms in the bathtub, signifying that Lavelle was now his girl.

Heather Lavelle came out of the gate fighting and was argumentative with us when we interviewed her.

We told her Savage had confessed and implicated her in Christian's murder, which angered her and motivated her to talk with us. She ultimately admitted to taking part in robbing and killing Christian. They both collectively agreed and confessed to the robbery, beating, and murder of Christian Rojas.

I'll never forget Lavelle as she revealed the brutal details of Christian's murder. She described that his screaming was so loud she turned on the water in the tub and stuck a rolled-up sock in his mouth to cover up the noise. When she realized Christian was finally dead, Lavelle's uncanny first thoughts included, "Well, I guess I can turn the water off now." She was insensitive, merciless, and completely unremorseful.

She and Savage had been in custody for several days, so we knew she wasn't using drugs. Depression is common among people battling an addiction to drugs or alcohol, and I think that Lavelle was suffering from it. Like Savage, Lavelle gave a signed confession admitting to robbing and killing Christian. Follow-up forensic testing also proved the blood on the brass knuckles was Christian's blood.

They had stolen the small safe from Christian's apartment and taken it back to Savage's house, where they had broken it open with tools. Lavelle knew Christian didn't trust banks and kept cash at home so he could send money to his family in Costa Rica. But much to their dismay, there was only $40 in the safe. They must have gotten to the safe in between Christian's paychecks. So they killed and tortured that young man for forty measly dollars. They also stole anything they could sell—tools, DVDs, etc.— for cash to buy drugs.

The Bucks County District Attorney's Office extradited Lavelle and Savage to Pennsylvania for prosecution. When their cases got to trial, they both pleaded guilty.

Eventually, Savage came to terms with what had happened and felt some remorse for the murder, unlike his counterpart. I had a small moment of sympathy for Savage in the courtroom when I saw him the day they were sentenced. We spoke, and he told me he deserved the death penalty and accepted that he might go to death row. Christian's family was very religious and did not believe in the death penalty, but they wanted to see justice served. Lavelle and Savage were both sentenced to life in prison without chance of parole.

Fast forward nine years to 2014. Lavelle was on stage giving a TED Talk from Muncy State Prison. While serving life in prison, she's learned to forgive herself and seems to be a role model inmate. This video is still available to see on YouTube.

I was interviewed by the producers of Investigation Discovery channel's television show *Nightmare Next Door* for the Christian Rojas murder story. My interviews were filmed inside the Bensalem Police Department, and we drove around town a little. The story was made into Episode 18 of Season 3 and aired in May 2013.

Then on March 1, 2020, Heather (my wife, not to be confused with Heather Lavelle) and I were out having dinner when my cell phone rang, displaying an unknown number from out of state. Naturally, I didn't think it was anyone of importance and figured it was another telemarketer trying to sell something. So I hit the button and sent the caller straight to voicemail. Later that evening, I noticed a message left in my inbox, and I decided to listen to it. I played it on speaker mode as my wife stood close by and listened in. It was a man's voice, very distinct, and it took me a minute to absorb it until he mentioned his name was Joe Kenda.

Kenda is a nineteen-year veteran of the Colorado Springs Police Department who retired in 1996. During his detective career, he made a lasting impression on a television producer who sought out Kenda for his documentary series *Homicide Hunter: Lt. Joe Kenda*. Heather is an avid and loyal fan of his show and has watched every single episode. She was in complete disbelief and repeatedly yelled, "You blew off Joe Kenda!" *Homicide Hunter* had since ended, but Kenda was then hosting a new series called *American Detective*.

The next day, I called Kenda back, and he answered. He talked about his current show, and I told him how much Heather loved him and *Homicide Hunter*. He was nice enough to send a few autographed things through the mail to Heather. He also asked me to participate in an episode of *American Detective*—my episode featuring the Christian Rojas murder aired on the Discovery Plus channel in May 2022. Unfortunately, due to the COVID-19 pandemic, I never got the chance to meet him in person. Kenda did his parts in a separate studio, and I was interviewed by an off-camera director—bummer.

CHAPTER 12
Barbara – Continued

It was about two years into our work on the Barbara Rowan case, and although we were making strides, we needed more to move forward. Mike Mosiniak and I prepared and delivered case evidence to the FBI Laboratory for DNA testing. A list of items included fingerprints, hair, clothing fibers, and tape for comparison testing. The hair and fibers had never been tested for DNA since DNA testing was unavailable until 1987. Again, detectives could not collect a rape kit on Barbara's remains due to the amount of decomposition of her body. Her shirt and bra, previously recovered as evidence from the crime scene in 1984, were submitted for fiber and DNA testing, along with her hair for DNA in 2004. Three years later, in 2007, the FBI laboratory examinations of the bra and blouse came back negative for any blood or semen.

I sent a letter to Lori Shaw's residence on February 27, 2008, asking if she would be willing to speak with me.

Two days later, she called me back at headquarters, and I explained who I was and why I was contacting her. She was pleasant and explained that she had split from George in 1999 and that they now had three daughters. According to Lori, George was very irresponsible, particularly as a father, and she told me that she had no contact with him anymore. She revealed that he had recently sent a card to one of their daughters and offered to get the address from the envelope for me. Thanks to Lori, I knew that George Shaw now lived in Geneva, Florida.

When asked if she thought George had killed Barbara Rowan, she replied, "I don't know; I hope not." In 1984, when the murder occurred, George told her he had nothing to do with it. And since he was her husband, she felt obligated to stand by her man, explained Lori. She remembered being interviewed by police in 1984 and meeting Barbara once before, but she never knew Barbara's parents.

Lori acknowledged that George was a meth user and dealer, and that Tom Genarro was his source of drugs. I asked if he ever got aggressive, particularly sexually aggressive, when he used drugs, and she told me he never got that way toward her. Lori had heard from people back in their old neighborhood that George was a "peeping Tom" and admitted she never really knew George as well as she should have. She had sympathy for Barbara Rowan's parents and felt they deserved closure. "Sometimes you don't see things when they're right under your nose," Lori disclosed. Lori denied knowing Robert Romanski, Bobby

Sanders, Billy Sanders, or William Wessler. However, she did acknowledge being friends with Dan Colacicco at one point because he was married to a woman who was best friends with George's sister. George had a secret life that Lori claimed she never knew about when they were married. "When he was drunk or high, he sometimes got emotional and cried," Lori recalled. Her daughter mentioned that he was recently diagnosed with diabetes and was still a heavy cigarette smoker to the best of her knowledge. Lori even offered to obtain one of his cigarette butts for DNA when he returned to Pennsylvania for a visit. She was accommodating and agreed to meet with Detective Cannon and me in the future, if needed.

Following this discussion, I tried to find a phone number connected with George Shaw. The only possible link discovered was a PO Box in Florida. I took a shot at it and sent a detailed letter on Police Department letterhead to the address, stating my reason for writing and leaving my phone number:

June 27, 2008
George F. Shaw
Re: Homicide Investigation 84-17505

Dear Mr. Shaw,

For the past several years, I have been working closely with the Forensics Laboratory of the FBI and working on unsolved or "cold" cases.

BENSALEM TOWNSHIP POLICE DEPARTMENT

2400 Byberry Road • Bensalem, PA 19020 • (215) 633-3700 • Fax (215) 633-3724

Frederick A. Harran
Director of Public Safety

June 27, 2008

George F. Shaw
PO Box 261
Geneva, FL 32732-0261

Re: Homicide Investigation 84-17505

Dear Mr. Shaw,

For the past several years I have been working closely with the Forensics Laboratory of the FBI and working on unsolved or "cold" cases.

Recently I have spoken to several old acquaintances of yours. I would very much like the opportunity to speak with you regarding the homicide of Barbara Rowan to clear up some issues.

Please contact me at your earliest convenience via telephone or email. My information is below

Thank you for your time and assistance in this matter.

Sincerely,

Detective Chris McMullin

Detective Chris McMullin #22238
Bensalem Police Department
2400 Byberry Rd.
Bensalem, PA 19020
215-633-3726
cmcmullin@bensalem-township.org

— Protect with honor, Serve with pride —

Letter to George Shaw

Recently I have spoken to several old acquaintances of yours. I would very much like the opportunity to speak with you regarding the homicide of Barbara Rowan to clear up some issues.

Please contact me at your earliest convenience via telephone or email. My information is below.

Thank you for your time and assistance in this matter.

Sincerely,
Detective Chris McMullin #22238
Bensalem Police Department
2400 Byberry Rd.
Bensalem, PA 19020

About a week later, on August 1, 2008, Shaw called after receiving my letter and left a voicemail. Of course, I saved the phone number he called from thanks to caller ID, and I called him back, identified myself, and asked how he was doing. He stated he had just returned from caring for his ill mother in Pennsylvania and was not doing well.

I cut to the chase and asked if he knew Bobby Sanders. He remembered the Sanders brothers from the Willow Grove area but stated he did not remember Litman, Romanski, or Sullivan.

Shaw immediately knew I was calling him about the Rowan case. He stated he had previously cooperated with the Bensalem Police and did everything they wanted him to do in 1984, including taking a lie detector (polygraph) test, which he passed. When I informed him that the results were, in fact, inconclusive rather than truthful, he became annoyed and replied, "Well, you Bensalem cops had it in for me."

Shaw recalled Barbara playing with his daughter but did not remember her father knocking on his door the night she went missing. I explained that Bobby Sanders remembered being with him at his apartment on Old Lincoln Highway when Mr. Rowan knocked on his door. Shaw adamantly denied Sanders being there and stated he never knew the Rowan family. I told him that Sanders had witnessed him enter the bedroom after Mr. Rowan left and heard some banging noises before Shaw exited the apartment and moved his car to the rear by the bedroom window. This time, Shaw remained silent. When asked if this was true, he replied, "I didn't do anything wrong." I asked again if it was true, and he answered, "No."

I told Shaw that the tape used to bind Barbara Rowan's hands, feet, and mouth was presently at the FBI Laboratory, being compared to the rolls of tape taken from his home and car in 1984. He was silent for a few seconds then replied, "Well, what do you want me to say about that?" I asked if he thought the tape from Barbara Rowan's body would match the tape retrieved from his home. Shaw was silent momentarily, then stated, "I don't see why it would." When I asked if he murdered Barbara Rowan, he replied, "I already told you I didn't do anything wrong." His voice cracked when he spoke, and he was nervous and upset. I asked Shaw if he had ever watched CSI and told him that technology had advanced since 1984. The call abruptly ended after I asked Shaw what he would do when I came to his door in the future.

On September 15, 2008, I telephoned the Seminole County Sheriff's Department and inquired if they covered

Geneva. The dispatcher stated that they covered parts of it. I asked if any of their detectives were on duty, but they had all left for the day. I left a message inquiring if they had had any contact with Shaw and if they could provide a residential address instead of a PO Box.

Two days later, Sergeant Brubaker of the Seminole County Sheriff's Department returned my call. I advised him of the investigation and explained that Shaw once lived in Bensalem and was now living in Geneva. Sergeant Brubaker informed me that his agency had contact with Shaw in 2006 when he had been accused of exposing himself to a minor.

In 2009, I received a letter from the FBI stating the tape retrieved from Barbara Rowan's body submitted for comparison in May of 2004 matched the tape recovered from Shaw's apartment in that they were alike in filament and fibers This commercial-grade tape was not available for retail and was manufactured exclusively by M&C Specialties in Southampton, Pennsylvania, where Dan Colacicco worked in 1984. Colacicco had told police that he gave Shaw rolls of tape from M&C Specialties.

Although decades later, things were homing in on Shaw once again. But this time, there was solid physical evidence to link Shaw to Barbara Rowan. And now Shaw was on Seminole County's radar as well. In the meantime, I found myself juggling another case that put Shaw on the back burner for some time.

One Saturday morning in July 2010, I was at work in my office and got called to the lobby. I met with a woman who told me that in 1999 she had filed a report about her ex-boyfriend, Walter Meyerle. She told me that Meyerle had sexually abused her daughter, who was only five years old back then. She explained that she didn't want her child being interviewed and having to testify in court at that age, so there was no investigation. Her daughter was now sixteen, the memories of the sexual abuse had resurfaced, and her daughter was now ready to face them.

After meeting with the victim's mother, I looked up her original report from 1999, but it didn't stop there. I then found three additional reports made against Meyerle between 2002 and 2003. All of the cases were still open. Meyerle had also been charged twice for making obscene phone calls. After learning about the other cases and reading the allegations, Meyerle went to the top of my priority list. I attempted to resurrect the old cases by reaching out to the victims. Not surprisingly, they were reluctant to speak with me after eight years had passed, and many of my phone calls went unanswered.

As for the most recent report against him, the sixteen-year-old victim failed to keep two appointments to discuss the case with me. I started an email dialogue with her to break the ice and, fortunately, it worked. She made disclosures that no child should ever have to endure. But I needed more than that to build a case against him.

In late October, I received a phone call from Detective Greg Biedler of the Bristol Township Police Department. Greg and I are friends and went to polygraph school together. Over the years, we became each other's "go-to guy" for our departments. When you need information or assistance from another agency, it's always much easier to have someone you can go to versus calling the agency cold and hoping a helpful person answers the phone. I answered the phone to a welcoming "Slappy!" which is a nickname Greg gave me back in polygraph school. It was short for "Slapnuts," undoubtedly a term of endearment, and I am forever grateful for the designation. Greg asked if anyone in my department had cases involving Walter Meyerle. I asked if he was screwin' with me, and he answered, "No, why?" I told him I had four open cases involving Meyerle as the alleged perpetrator, dating back to 2002. Greg had recently caught a case involving Meyerle as the suspect and had an angle. We immediately met and compared notes, and it then turned into a joint investigation. Not long after that, we sought the help of Detective Tim Perkins from the district attorney's office and Assistant District Attorney Jennifer Schorn.

Both Tim and Jennifer also fell into the "go-to" category. Tim was a former Bristol Township detective, and he and Greg were good friends. Jennifer had been my first choice "go-to" prosecutor for several years. We had worked together on a few homicide cases, and her dedication, knowledge, ability, and passion for helping victims were—and still are—remarkable.

We now had five abuse victims. Since Meyerle had been around a while, the potential for more victims was very high. We both agreed Jennifer should be at the helm for this one. The team was formed, and after a long and intense investigation, Meyerle was arrested on St. Patrick's Day, 2011. We charged him with sexually assaulting eighteen victims, as well as possession of child pornography. He didn't make bail, and not long after being incarcerated, he attempted a prison escape. In August 2012, he was convicted in a waiver trial and sentenced to 484.5 to 984.5 years. This was a record sentence in Pennsylvania. Meyerle is a predator who preys on those he manipulates. There is a special place in hell for him, too.

After this investigation, I recruited Jennifer for the Barbara Rowan case. I gave her a copy of the Rowan file over lunch and asked if she would work on the case with Detective Mosiniak and me. I explained that I believed the case was solvable. After reading the file, Jennifer was also dedicated to solving the homicide and agreed to take on the case.

Jennifer and I were both inundated with other cases, so a few years passed, and, unfortunately, the Rowan case continued to wait. But in March of 2015, Jennifer called and asked for my thoughts on putting the Barbara Rowan case into the investigating grand jury. I immediately said yes and asked what she needed.

Finally, it was going to move forward! An investigating grand jury is like a trial jury in that it comprises people from the community who are selected to serve. However, the grand jurors are chosen randomly and may serve for 18 months to two years. They meet only once a week, as opposed to daily. The purpose of the investigative grand jury is not to determine whether a person is guilty or not guilty or whether they committed the crime in question but whether there is ample evidence to bring forth charges for prosecution. An investigative grand jury makes the initial determination about whether there is enough evidence to constitute probable cause that a crime has been committed and to charge a person with that crime. An investigative grand jury only needs probable cause to return a presentment. If the investigative grand jury decided to recommend Shaw should be charged, he would be arrested and have a preliminary hearing. At the preliminary hearing, the prosecution would have to show that there is sufficient evidence that a crime was committed and that it is more than likely that the defendant committed the crime. This is called prima facie. *Prima facie* is a Latin expression that means "based on first impression." Whether the defendant is guilty or not guilty is not established at the preliminary hearing level. If the prosecution succeeds at this level, the case proceeds to the court of common pleas, where the fact finder(s) renders a verdict of guilty or not guilty. At this level, the defendant can plead guilty or have a trial by a judge or jury. A trial by judge is called a bench trial or a waiver trial, where only a judge is the fact finder and renders a verdict, whereas a trial by jury is when twelve citizens are the fact finders and render a verdict.

We created a PowerPoint presentation to give the grand jury a clear idea about the case. Then we contacted the Montgomery County District Attorney's Office to retrieve courtroom transcripts and files on Shaw's home invasion rape case in October 1984. Jennifer needed every record of Shaw's prior bad acts and behavior. She used to have a couple of good contacts in the Montgomery County DA's office, but they had all moved on, and she no longer had a "go-to" person. I, on the other hand, did.

Flashback to December of 2014, two suspects wearing masks robbed a coins and collectibles store in Bensalem. They tied up the employees and one customer, then smashed out the display cases, stealing thousands of dollars' worth of coins. I hadn't worked on this type of case since working in the Special Victims Unit. On the day this call came over the police radio, another SVU detective named Kevin Cornish and I looked at each other and figured, "What the hell?" So we headed to the scene and watched the robbers commit the robbery on store video. As the robbers exited the store, one of the suspects removed his mask and looked right up at the camera as he walked out. No one recognized the suspect, however. We decided to use facial recognition software to identify him, but that took a little time. So we employed a second high-tech yet innovative police method by putting his photo on the news.

I was emotionally and mentally in a very dark place during this time. My personal life sucked, and I felt empty inside. I was depressed, alone, and somewhat isolated at times. I was going through a phase of being "gun shy" in all aspects of my life. There was also some turmoil at work from a group of toxic employees, which reduced morale and made work miserable to go to every day.

The following day, after airing the robbery suspect's photo on the news, I went to work, and there was a voicemail on my phone. I didn't know it at the time, but not only would that message lead to a massive break in the case, it would also lead to a huge break in my life.

I had been bombarded with a ton of things from the moment I walked into headquarters, so I didn't listen to the message right away. It took about an hour before I finally got to my voicemail, and when I did, I heard a lovely voice. It started, "Good evening, detective, my name is Heather Hines, and I'm an assistant district attorney in Montgomery County." She had my attention before I even knew what she was calling for. Her message went on to say that she had seen the story on the news about the robbery and had information about the suspect.

I called her back immediately, and she dropped what she was doing to talk with me. She provided a lot of vital information, and with her help and the help of other Montgomery County officers, we were able to identify both robbery suspects.

Heather knew one of the suspects from a robbery case she was prosecuting in Montgomery County. He had been released from jail and was out on bail. The fact that he was out on bail from her case and committed another robbery in Bucks County infuriated her. She was willing to assist us however she could and gave me the contact information for a probation officer supervising the other suspect, who she had also helped us identify.

We learned, through the probation officer, that due to the suspect's poor financial credit, his financing company had put a GPS tracker on his car in case they had to repossess it. With the help of the finance company, we tracked the vehicle to Atlantic City, New Jersey.

The chase was on, and four of us—Kevin Cornish, me, and two other officers were headed to Atlantic City. Unfortunately, the other two officers were involved in an automobile accident so only two of us made it there. Thankfully, the officers were not injured, but their car was not operable. They waited for the tow truck while Kevin and I kept going. We got to Atlantic City and found the robbers' vehicle, hotel, and pawn shops where they had sold some stolen coins, but we didn't find them. They had ditched their truck, and, at this point, their whereabouts were unknown. We kept our feelers out, waiting for a new lead.

I called and texted Heather to keep her in the loop. One afternoon, I got up from my desk, and Kevin asked, "Where are you going?" I answered, "To the men's room, if that's okay with you." Kevin didn't miss a beat and, in his typical, ball-breaking fashion, said, "Don't forget to text Heather and let her know." Kevin had noticed my strong connection with Heather.

About a week later, we received information about our suspects pawning more coins in Baltimore, Maryland. Later that same day, the suspects were robbed in Philadelphia, resulting in one of them getting shot. The robbers who had brutally victimized the people in the coin store were now victims themselves.

The suspect who was shot survived and was taken to a nearby hospital in Philadelphia. The second suspect escaped, but police caught up with him a day later at his mother's house in Chester County, Pennsylvania. He confessed to everything. After we finished the interview, Kevin said, "You gotta call Heather and tell her we caught them." He knew I would do precisely that, but he just wanted to keep breaking my balls.

I informed Heather that both suspects had been captured, and she was relieved. She had scheduled a hearing to revoke bail on their robbery case from Montgomery County and asked if I wanted to make a "cameo appearance" in court to testify about what the suspects had done in Bucks County while they were out on bail. Finally, this was my chance to meet Heather in person, so I agreed and asked that she send me a subpoena.

The following week I was off to court in Montgomery County. When Kevin got wind of where I was going, he said, "Don't blow it!" I told him I had reviewed our reports and would be fine. He replied, "Not your testimony, stupid—don't blow it with Heather!" I pretended I had no idea why he would say such a thing, but that was a complete and utter lie. I had never testified in Montgomery County and was unfamiliar with the courthouse, so Heather gave me the address and parking instructions. She told me to text her when I entered the lobby, and she would meet me there. If we are lucky, we only have a few moments in life that are beautiful, perfect, and unforgettable. I experienced one of those moments when Heather stepped off the elevator: Breathe, pause, take it in, and enjoy it. In my mind, I returned to the Rollerama skating rink in the summer of 1984 while the song "Waiting for a Girl Like You" by Foreigner played during a couples-only skate. It was perfect.

The court hearing was productive, and bail for our common defendants was revoked. I considered the victory bittersweet since this case was what was keeping Heather and me communicating and seeing each other. Now that the bail hearing was over, there were no more excuses to see or even talk with her.

When I returned to headquarters, Kevin asked how it went. "All good, bail revoked," I answered. He replied, "Yeah, I figured that, stupid. How did it go with your new best friend?" Kevin could tell right away that I was preoccupied with meeting Heather. He was a great, good-hearted detective, but this took little detecting.

Sadly, a few weeks later, in late January 2015, Kevin had a massive heart attack and passed away while participating in a 5K run for charity. He was only forty-two years old. We were all stunned and saddened by this tragic news. I miss working with him, and I miss him as a friend. We all do.

In the meantime, Heather and I kept in touch by phone and met for coffee now and then. With the Barbara Rowan case back on the table, I followed Jennifer's suggestion and contacted the Montgomery County DA's Office. I phoned Heather specifically to request access to the trial records from Shaw's 1985 rape case. She was more than happy to help, and later that week, Jennifer and I planned to meet her at the DA's office. She helped tremendously and provided us with all the documents we needed there. While Jennifer and I worked through all the files and made copies, I would occasionally catch a glimpse of Heather walking by, and we would make eye contact and smile. Who was I kidding? I was crazy about this girl.

After Jennifer and I left the building, she gave me a ride to my car. While pulling out of the parking garage, she looked at me and said, "I think that girl likes you," which put a smile on my face. Later that night, Heather sent a text asking me what I was up to. I got ballsy and responded, "Waiting for your address so I can come to see you." The next thing I knew, I was driving an hour to her house. I was nervous during the entire commute because we'd never been alone together. She kissed me first, and we've been inseparable ever since. We were connected in a way that was anything but ordinary. Although our case-solving chapter had ended, an extraordinary new chapter had begun, and I married my best friend on March 25, 2017.

CHAPTER 13
Investigating Grand Jury

On July 3, 2015, I checked social media for involved persons related to Barbara Rowan's investigation and located Bobby Sanders on Facebook. But after screening all seventy of his friends for possible links to George Shaw, I could not trace anything.

In the meantime, Mike, Jennifer, and I held prep meetings with retirees Dave Rouland, Bill Koszarek, retired Chief Ted Sajak, and some of the witnesses from 1984. We picked the brains of the original detectives in the Rowan case and listened to how they felt during their time with the investigation. Their interactions with Shaw and gut feelings about the case were vital. They shared their opinions, including where they believed there were weaknesses in the case that had prevented it from being solved. Each of them felt Shaw was "the guy" and that the Rowan murder was solvable.

During this same time, a friend lost a family member who went missing for five days. On the fifth day, the family contacted a spiritual medium named Theresa Roba. Roba told the family they would find him that same day—which they did.

I wanted to speak to the same medium about the Rowan case. I only contacted her on Facebook using my first name, knowing I had virtually no information on my profile—not even a photo. She replied, and we set up a conference by telephone. The day we spoke, she never asked where I worked. I didn't give her any personal information, but I did tell her I was a detective working on a case. (I didn't mention it was a cold case). She refused to take any money from me and genuinely wanted to help me.

Roba proclaimed, "I have a young lady here with me with long auburn hair who wants to say thank you and wants her family to know she's okay." She stated, "This happened a very long time ago, didn't it?" She said, "The person responsible for this is in the South." Then she ended with, "Did you talk to the mechanic? You should talk to the mechanic." This experience was so surreal; I was shocked. I immediately scheduled an appointment with Al Gougler, owner of Al's Used Auto Parts, the following week.

A few days later, I spoke with Gougler, who had been Shaw's landlord and lived across the street from him in 1984. Gougler still owned the shop on Old Lincoln Highway, across the street from where the Shaws lived. He mentioned that he and his family knew Barbara and often saw her going to Shaws' apartment.

When I asked him if Barbara ever babysat for the Shaws, he replied, "Absolutely, she babysat for the Shaws." He had observed Barbara going into the Shaws' apartment constantly and watched George and Lori leave without Kelly. It was obvious to him that Barbara was babysitting their daughter. Gougler described Barbara as being raised poor: "Although she was somewhat immature, she was a nice girl and well-mannered."

Gougler disclosed that he had no doubts Shaw tried something on her and killed her. Unfortunately, the Shaws were month-to-month renters, so they had no long-term ties to their lease when they suddenly moved out. Detectives never asked Gougler in 1984 if Barbara Rowan was the Shaws' babysitter. Identifying Barbara as their babysitter built more evidence against Shaw. It's clear that Gougler was the mechanic Roba spoke of.

The following week, on July 16, 2015, Detective Mosiniak and I presented the Rowan case before the investigating grand jury at the Bucks County Courthouse. We both testified about Barbara's disappearance and the ultimate discovery of her remains. Additionally, retired Detective Sergeants Tidwell and Duntzee of the Upper Moreland Police Department testified about the disclosures made to them over the years by both Billy and Bobby Sanders about Shaw's involvement in the Rowan murder. We were scheduled to return to the grand jury on September 3, 2015.

Our next stop was Stroudsburg in Monroe County, Pennsylvania, where Bobby Sanders lived with his girlfriend of fifteen years, Donna Zabroski. By this time, we knew Sanders was out of prison, and that he and Zabroski were splitting up. Dave Nieves and John Monaghan were two detectives I had hand-picked to assist us because I knew they would deliver. Wendy Bentzoni is a sharp detective from Monroe County who also helped us with the case.

We initially spent our time tailing both Sanders and Zabroski. We followed Zabroski everywhere, including her job, and by the end of it all, we had her daily schedule down to a science. We even knew what time she took her cigarette breaks at work.

Detective Bentzoni created a fake Facebook profile as an attractive female and messaged Bobby Sanders. He eagerly responded, and they began a friendly dialogue. A seductive invite to meet her at a nearby bar would reel Sanders in and lead us to him. Mosiniak and I were nearby and located him walking up the street to meet the mysterious woman. We stopped on the side of the road, greeted him, and got reacquainted with him. He remembered us and was not happy to see us. He reluctantly agreed to accompany us to the Monroe County detective's office, where we interviewed him. But, again, he wouldn't give any additional information and refused to talk anymore before discussing things with his girlfriend. We then ended the interview.

On September 1, 2015, we again saw Sanders and Zabroski. We planned to interview them both simultaneously, so Sanders couldn't continue dodging our questions by saying he needed to talk to his girlfriend before telling the truth. Unfortunately, the interviews did not produce a confession from Sanders or any corroborating information from Zabroski. She played dumb the entire time and made ambiguous statements claiming she was trying to recall what Sanders had told her—"I'm trying to recall what Bob said to me, but all I can remember is that he and a friend did something terrible. After a while, he told me about a little girl but not exactly what happened to her. I wish I could remember more, but I can't now; I'm sorry."

I reviewed her Facebook page and noticed that she played strange murder mystery games all the time. Was this a subconscious cry for help? Ultimately, we would find out. We served Sanders and Zabroski with subpoenas to the investigating grand jury.

Right before the grand jury case, weird things started happening to me. For instance, one day, I was driving to my barber in Hatboro, sitting at a red light on County Line Road. I looked to my right and saw a school named St. John Bosco. I then realized that's where Shaw went to school. The traffic light turned green then, and I drove to the next red light. Much to my surprise, I looked to my left and saw a big box truck that said "Shaw" across the side of it. Creepy things like that made me wonder if there were greater forces at work, and they continued to happen.

One day I was sitting in Jennifer's office. She had received an email from someone regarding a different case—a medical release form requested previously for a doctor's office to send medical records on behalf of a victim. Jennifer pointed out the unusual name of the office employee who acknowledged receipt of the release form—her name was "Patricia Rowan," the name of Barbara Rowan's mother. However, they were not the same individual. Creepy, indeed.

On September 3, 2015, Sanders reluctantly appeared at the investigative grand jury. While on the stand, he was initially evasive and belligerent, but after Jennifer reminded him that he was under oath, he finally came clean and testified truthfully about the evening of August 3, 1984. He stated that Shaw owed him money and would pay him back by providing him meth to use that night at Shaw's apartment. He told the grand jury that while he and Shaw were driving to Shaw's apartment, Shaw said that a babysitter was watching his daughter and that he had "slipped her a little something to make her feel relaxed." Sanders testified that when they arrived and he entered Shaw's apartment, he saw Barbara Rowan there. He described her as a young teenage girl with long red hair and glasses. Sanders stated that Shaw gave him some meth, took Barbara into the bedroom, and shut the door. Sanders testified that he stayed in the living room to get high. A few minutes later, a man knocked on the front door of Shaw's apartment, and Sanders spoke with him. He said the man was looking for his daughter and asked if she was inside, to which Sanders answered, "No." He said the man seemed agitated and angry and said he was calling the police as he left.

Sanders heard some unusual sounds from the bedroom during that time, but then they stopped. Shortly after that, Shaw came out of the bedroom alone, profusely sweating, and completely disheveled in appearance. He stated to Sanders, "I fucked up." Sanders then looked into Shaw's bedroom and observed Barbara's lifeless body on the bed. Shaw had assaulted and strangled Barbara to death in the bedroom of his home while his three-year-old daughter was asleep in the other bedroom and while Mr. Rowan had been standing before the door asking Sanders if she was in the apartment. Sanders claimed he was scared to death of Shaw and helped him out of fear for his own life. He assisted Shaw with putting Barbara's body in the trunk of Shaw's car and discarding her on the side of northbound Route 1.

Throughout his testimony, I twirled my Nan's Claddagh ring that I kept on a necklace. I was ecstatic—we finally got the truth from Sanders, and I will never forget that day. The investigating grand jury returned a presentment at the end of the day. Jennifer said to Mike and me, "We're charging."

On September 10, 2015, Zabroski testified in front of the grand jury. It was evident that Zabroski was dishonest, and the grand jury would need to take a recess. She repeatedly told the court that she couldn't remember anything Sanders had told her. Detective Nieves and I walked Zabroski into the hallway of the courthouse, and we calmly asked, "Donna, if you had knowledge about this little girl's murder, would you be reluctant to admit this because you're afraid you will be punished for knowing about it all this time and never telling anybody?" At first, she didn't reply and glared at us with a flat, passive stare. We tried to reassure her that she would not be in trouble for failing to report what Sanders had told her in the past. But our words still did not change Zabroski's demeanor. I strongly felt this hindered her ability to be truthful on the stand. So I sought out Jennifer and told her what was happening.

Jennifer met Zabroski in the hallway and spoke to her with sincerity and empathy. Zabroski admitted she was not being honest in the courtroom for fear of getting in trouble since she failed to report to the police the knowledge she possessed fourteen years ago. Jennifer explained that she had not committed a crime. Possession of such knowledge, even if it was about a heinous murder, is not a crime, and Jennifer reiterated there would be no legal consequences if she told the truth on the stand that day.

Zabroski re-entered the courtroom very emotionally and went back on the stand. On record, Jennifer explained to the court what she had discussed with Zabroski, Detective Nieves, and me in the hallway. Zabroski struggled morally with the revolting nature of Barbara's murder, especially since she was a mother and grandmother herself. The deeper Jennifer dove into the questioning, the more Zabroski became visibly emotional. Subsequently, Zabroski's testimony was nothing short of mind-blowing.

The courtroom watched intently as she struggled to divulge the gut-wrenching details Sanders had told her years prior. When Jennifer approached Zabroski on the stand with crime scene photos of Barbara, she became ill with emotion. Zabroski began sobbing uncontrollably and, at times, physically retching and gasping on the witness stand.

She recollected what Sanders had told her, explaining, "He was shooting up dope in the chair, and there was a young girl there who came to the house to babysit." She couldn't remember where Barbara had gone, but she wasn't in the room where Sanders was. "Whatever room the little girl went into, she never came out, and George came out of the same room not looking good... he was sweaty." Zabroski continued, "When George came out of the room, he asked Bobby to help him and something about the car that was moved from the front of the house to the back, and Bobby helped George get rid of her body." That statement from Sanders made it clear to her that the babysitter was dead. Zabroski continued to disclose additional details Sanders had told her, such as "the little girl's hands being tied behind her back" and how he "helped George place the body of the dead little girl in the trunk of George's car." Zabroski even knew about the little girl's father, who came looking for her that night.

Zabroski described Sanders as visually upset when he told her the story fourteen years ago. "He wasn't bragging about it but was more scared of being caught and going back to jail," Donna said. She also admitted to fearing Sanders during the early years of their relationship because of his criminal history and his involvement with a motorcycle gang. On many occasions, Zabroski tried to convince Sanders to do the right thing and tell the police the truth about what had happened, but Sanders continued to blow it off.

Shortly after Zabroski's grand jury testimony, we met with Danny Green. He was an excellent eyewitness and agreed to testify in the trial. In 1984, he and his wife were vital witnesses, but unfortunately, nothing came out of it. Sadly, Mrs. Green passed away before the trial. It was her statement that identified the unique Rebel Soldier type of hat that Sanders used to wear and was wearing on the night of Barbara Rowan's murder. She described it as a painter's cap. Mr. Green testified to what he had observed that night, and he authenticated his late wife's statement.

CHAPTER 14
Meeting Shaw In Florida

After the testimony of Sanders and Zabroski before the investigating grand jury, we had probable cause to arrest Shaw for the rape and murder of Barbara Rowan. On September 28, 2015, Detective Mosiniak and I flew down and met with Jennifer Spears, a Seminole County Sheriff's Office (SCSO) detective.

Spears is one of about ten detectives who are all part of the SCSO's cold-case squad. She was very proactive and had researched Shaw, keeping him on her radar. We initially planned to go to his house and ask him to return to the Sheriff's Office to speak with us about the Rowan case. Then we would present him with a subpoena to the investigating grand jury in Bucks County, PA. However, after consulting with the state attorney in Seminole County, we learned it wouldn't be enforced. Florida will not compel one of its citizens to be subpoenaed out of state for self-incrimination purposes. In other words, a judge in Florida would not order Shaw to report to the investigating grand jury in Bucks County, PA. Spears and her team were heading to where Shaw lived, and Mosiniak and I followed.

After our ride, we found ourselves at the end of a long, lonely dirt road with chickens running around. We parked about two hundred feet away from an old shanty trailer known to be Shaw's residence. There was a small front porch with steps and a folding chair at the top of the landing. Shaw was sitting right there with a big ugly belly hanging over his shorts and no shoes on. We planned to make it seem like he was not the primary suspect and just talk to him in a non-custodial interview. While Spears and her team waited, Mosiniak and I walked up and introduced ourselves as detectives from Bucks County and explained our reason for being there. "We just want to talk about the [Barbara Rowan] case and take a formal statement from you," I clarified. Shaw was caught off guard and visibly nervous. I had spoken to him on the phone eight years before, but it appeared as though he didn't recognize my name.

When we asked Shaw why he had moved to Florida, he acted very surprised. He replied, "You don't know why I moved to Florida?" We answered, "No." At that point, he casually admitted, "I killed someone." He then told us that while working at a construction job site in Pennsylvania, he had run over and killed another construction worker with a large piece of machinery he was driving. That case was deemed accidental by OSHA and was supposedly Shaw's reason for moving to Florida.

I revealed that I was a Bensalem detective, which annoyed him. "One of your guys called me about eight years ago and was an asshole while making all kinds of threats about the Rowan murder," Shaw stated. He hadn't the slightest clue that the "asshole" he was referring to was me.

At that moment, he slowly stood up, attempted to force his way by us, and announced, "We're done here." As he reached for the front door, Mosiniak and I took him down on his front porch and attempted to handcuff him. Shaw struggled with us, but we quickly overpowered him and handcuffed him. We then told Shaw we had a warrant for his arrest for the murder of Barbara Rowan. The authorities in Florida then charged Shaw as a "fugitive of justice." This charge enabled them to imprison him until Bucks County authorities arranged his extradition back to Pennsylvania.

Once at the Sheriff's Office, Shaw was given his Miranda warnings before being questioned. During the interview, I noticed he had a tattoo on his arm with a cross and a date. I asked about it, and he explained it was in memory of his father. Shaw refused to speak with us after that and stated that his attorney would speak for him. The interview then ended.

Since I had never contacted the Rowans about reopening the case, I knew we had to alert them as to what had happened. News of Shaw's arrest would hit the press within the next twenty-four hours, and we knew we had to work quickly to prevent them from being blindsided.

Mosiniak made the call to the Rowans. Patricia Rowan answered, and Mosiniak introduced himself. There was a pause, and she asked, "Are you calling about my daughter?" Mosiniak replied, "Yes, I am." After a few seconds of silence, Mrs. Rowan replied, "I have been waiting thirty-one years for this phone call." Mosiniak explained that there had been an arrest in Florida for Barbara's murder and there would be a second arrest soon to follow (Sanders). He also informed the Rowans of the imminent press conference scheduled to take place with the local TV news stations.

After Mike called the Rowans, I called retired detectives Bill Koszarek and Dave Rouland. It was as much their arrest as it was ours. They were thrilled. They, too, had waited thirty-one years for this moment.

The press conference took place the next day, October 2, 2015. Robert and Patricia Rowan elected not to attend. I met Jennifer Schorn and Mike Mosiniak outside the police department, and we walked into the press conference together. KYW-TV's investigative reporter, Walt Hunter, asked me for a statement. I said, "I'm just glad we got to this point; this is about Barbara and her family." All major Philadelphia news networks—including channels 3, 6, and 10—were there filming. Bensalem Director of Public Safety Fred Harran, Mayor Joseph DiGirolamo, and District Attorney David Heckler were also present.

After the press conference, the three of us and a representative from NOVA (Network of Victim Assistance) all went to the Rowan home in Bensalem. We discussed our work on the case over the past thirteen years and the extradition process for Shaw. Patricia Rowan's sister, brother-in-law, and their two daughters, Barbara's cousins, were present. The entire Rowan family was sobbing tears of joy, as expected. We explained the investigation and brought them up to speed on what else to expect.

Shaw arrived in Pennsylvania to be arraigned a few days later. The Rowans were present at his arraignment. By Pennsylvania law, there is no bail for murder; therefore, Shaw was committed to the Bucks County Prison until his preliminary hearing. The court constables took him into custody and placed him into their handcuffs and shackles, at which time they removed my set of handcuffs. Fred Harran asked for my handcuffs, which I handed over to him, and he, in turn, gave them to Mr. and Mrs. Rowan as a symbol of solidarity.

If you ever doubt the power of making a positive difference in someone or something else's life, I always reference a poem titled *The Starfish Story* by Loren Eiseley:

> *There's this old man walking up and down the beach with all of these starfish lying on the beach, dying after a storm. A young man was picking them up and throwing them back into the ocean. "Why do you bother?" the old man scoffed. "You're not saving enough to make a difference." The young man picked up another starfish and sent it spinning back to the water. "Made a difference to that one," he replied.* You can make a difference every day. (Eisley, 1969, adapted from *The Star Thrower*)

The reasons why you would reopen a cold case? You owe it to the victim(s) and the families, and when a homicide goes unsolved, a killer is walking freely among us; we owe it to society to prevent more people from becoming their victims. We made a positive difference to the Rowan family.

After the arrests of Shaw and Sanders in 2015, the Vidocq Society called and said they wanted to present us with the Vidocq Society Medal of Honor. The Vidocq Society, as mentioned earlier in the book, is an elite members-only, crime-solving club in Philadelphia, founded in 1990. In 2015, I was not a member—so I was thrilled when I got the invite!

The Vidocq Society held its annual banquet in October 2015. It was a top-notch, black-tie event at the breathtaking Pen Ryn Mansion on the Delaware River in Bensalem. My friend and mentor, Frank Friel, had passed by this time. It was unfortunate that he could not be there to share in this special occasion.

When Vidocq Society founder William Fleischer presented us with our medals,, he told me that Frank was looking down from Heaven and was very proud. After all, if it weren't for Frank giving me a shot, I wouldn't have been there to begin with. It was an honor to be presented with the Vidocq Society Medal of Honor for solving the Barbara Rowan case, and a night to remember. But the investigation wasn't over yet. We still had to convict Shaw.

CHAPTER 15
The Investigation Continues

A big misconception many people have is that after a suspect is arrested for a murder, the investigation is over. Nothing could be further from the truth. Shaw and Sanders were arrested and in custody, but the investigation continued.

On October 8, 2015, Detective Mosiniak and I went to the home of Luther Sanders in Upper Moreland. Luther had recently passed away, and the house was under the care of Linda Boller, a family friend. Pursuant to a search warrant, we collected some items, including rebel soldier hats that belonged to Bobby Sanders. These rebel soldier hats were significant to the case because they matched the type of hat that Mrs. Green described one of the men wearing the night she and her husband observed the two men on the side of the road where Barbara's body was found. We needed to show that Bobby Sanders collected and wore this style hat.

Many years prior, Linda had lived with Bobby's brother, Bill. She had kicked him out because of his excessive alcohol abuse but remained friendly with the rest of the family. Bill's alcoholism progressively worsened, leading to health complications and eventually his death.

When they had first begun dating twenty-two years prior, Bill had told Linda that he and his brother knew of a murder. Bill mentioned very few details to her but did indicate that the victim was a young girl or a babysitter. She assumed he was referring to a biker murder or a drug deal gone wrong since they were both "biker wannabes."

Shaw's ex-wife, Lori, is now remarried and goes by Lori Keefe. My initial interaction with her in 2004 was a positive experience. Back then, she was cooperative and willing to go out of her way to contact us if she heard when George would be in town again. But we never got that call. In 2015, Lori did not want to be dragged back into the investigation and was no longer cooperative. In 1984, The Pontiac LeMans was registered to her name (both of their cars were), but the LeMans suddenly vanished, and no record of it was ever found except for a traffic ticket George was issued while driving it in July of 1984. Lori was very inconsistent with her story and the information she provided. She claimed she had no idea what happened to the car and could never give us a straight answer when asked if the vehicle had been sold or dumped. She repeatedly contradicted her statements from 1984. A car is a significant asset to most people, and I didn't believe that Lori didn't know what had happened to it.

On October 15, 2015, Lori Keefe finally testified under oath before the grand jury. Jennifer Schorn began with questions about Lori's previous marriage to George Shaw. They had ended their fourteen-year marriage in 1994. Lori told the grand jury that George moved to Florida in 2005 and had a minimal relationship with their children, leaving her to raise the three girls on her own.

Lori and George grew up in the same neighborhood and began dating when she was seventeen. She knew George was a drug user then and admitted to using drugs herself. They both mainly snorted methamphetamine initially, eventually progressing to injecting the drug. She claimed they stopped using drugs when she learned she was pregnant with Kelly. This was before they were married in 1980.

Lori recalled the three of them living in the Diplomat Apartments when Kelly was just a toddler. At one point, before the summer of 1984, Lori gave George an ultimatum when she learned he was doing drugs again. She remembered, on one occasion, coming home from work at around half past midnight to an apartment filled with people who were using drugs, including George. All of this took place with their baby girl in the apartment. Lori said she would not have her daughter raised in an environment of drugs, so she packed up Kelly and their belongings and moved into her mother's house. But this separation was short-lived, and in a few days, they reconciled. The move to the red house in Trevose was mainly to get George away from his drug associates. Lori borrowed a car from her parents to drive herself to and from work in Horsham. That car was a Chevy Impala. They also had a fully operable red 1973 Pontiac LeMans Sport that Lori stated George typically drove. She described the LeMans as having a white hard-top roof and white interior. Lori claimed the only time that car was disabled was before they moved. She confirmed it was fully operable while they were living in Trevose. This again contradicted previous statements. Decision Data was her employer, and her regular work schedule was the second shift from 4:00 p.m. to 12:30 a.m., Monday through Friday.

Lori refuted George's 1984 statements to police that he drove her to and from work daily. She stated that it made no sense for him to drive her to and from work when she had a car to drive herself. She did agree that George would occasionally bring Kelly to her job during her lunch break.

During this time, Lori thought George had cleaned up his act and stopped using drugs. She did not know he was still using meth because he was not doing it in her presence. It wasn't until later she discovered he was back to using drugs, but she said she did not know he was selling it.

At this point, Jennifer reminded Lori of her recent statement to detectives that she had learned George was back to using and selling drugs. With a stern examination by Jennifer, Lori finally admitted to knowing about George selling drugs to make money early on in their relationship.

Lori was also aware that Barbara would often come to the apartment to play with their three-year-old daughter while she was at work. She was also aware of the age difference between Barbara and Kelly.

After a brief recess, the court reconvened, with Lori back on the stand. Jennifer revisited the time when Lori gave George the ultimatum just before she left him. This was confirmed as occurring in the spring of 1984, but Lori could not recall exactly when. Lori admitted that she knew when George was using meth from the change in his demeanor and behavior. Lori also stated they had left the red house apartment at the end of August and gone to live with her parents in neighboring Montgomery County.

The next day—October 16, 2015—Detective Mosiniak and I interviewed Vanessa Montevale. In 1984, she was eighteen and often hung out with Kim Sullivan at McDonald's in Hatboro. Montevale recalled meeting George on one occasion at an apartment across from the Red Stallion bar. She couldn't remember who took her there, but that person introduced her to George. From what Montevale could recollect, George's wife and child were not in the apartment. She admitted to having a drug problem back then and, at the time, snorted methamphetamine. She and George snorted the drug together in that apartment, and Montevale identified George's face from a photo we showed her. She remembered that he went into the bathroom and "shot up."

In November 1984, police interviewed Montevale and stated that she had been left alone with George, and he had made some sort of sexual advance toward her, making her feel very uncomfortable. She struggled to remember but vaguely recalled that he may have locked the front door. This triggered an urgent feeling of "needing to get out of there." She panicked, made an excuse to leave, and ran out of the apartment. That was the only time she was in George's company; she did not remember seeing him after that incident. When Detective Mosiniak and I showed her a photo of Bobby Sanders, Montevale said his name and face appeared familiar, but nothing else stood out about him.

Montevale recalled hearing about George's alleged involvement with a little girl's murder in 1984. She remembered thinking how lucky she was to get away that eerie day at George's apartment. Throughout the interview, Montevale repeatedly emphasized how frightened she felt at that apartment with George.

In November 2015, Mosiniak and I paid a visit to George's daughter, Kelly, who was, at the time, incarcerated in Montgomery County. She was thirty-four. After telling her who we were, she agreed to speak with us. Kelly didn't want to believe her father had killed Barbara. Kelly vaguely remembered Barbara, and her mother had told her a somewhat altered version of events when she was a little older. The relationship between Kelly and her father in 2015 was okay, according to Kelly, contradicting what Lori had told detectives in a previous interview that "George was an absent father." Later, during her father's trial, she publicly addressed the Rowan family and apologized for their loss. I'm sure she was emotionally torn, knowing she was the little girl Barbara was babysitting when she was brutally raped and murdered.

Daniel Colacicco and his wife Ellen agreed to be re-interviewed by Detective Mosiniak and me at their residence on December 11, 2015. As we spoke more in-depth with Daniel, we learned that he and George had been friends, beginning around their teenage years. Their parents lived diagonally across from each other then, so they became buddies. Daniel met his wife of twenty-five years, Ellen, at George and Lori Shaw's wedding. At that time, Ellen was good friends with George's sister, Debbie. Later, Debbie relocated to Florida, and most of their communication occurred through Facebook. Sometimes they would get together when the Shaws returned to Philadelphia for special occasions.

Daniel recalled initial interviews with detectives in 1984 about working for M&C Specialties. He was employed there for three years and then quit in June 1984. His responsibilities mainly included rewinding tape from big rolls into smaller sizes on machinery. "M&C did not manufacture the tape, but they received it in large tubes, and everybody sliced it down to different specifications," Daniel explained. However, M&C Specialties made other types of tape, including duct tape, said Daniel. It was likely that boxes of defective tape were brought home by employees back in 1984. Daniel verified that he had given some of the duct tape to George and other friends. Mosiniak and I questioned him about the statement he gave detectives in 1984 when George was initially a suspect. He could not recall it, so we read him the original transcribed statement he had previously given detectives to jog his memory. The record showed that Daniel had told detectives George had approached him during the investigation, stating, "I've been giving you a lot of thought about the tape."

Upon questioning Daniel about what he may have heard on the street in 1984 relative to the alleged murder, he could not recall or provide any feedback. He denied ever discussing the Rowan murder case with George or having any knowledge about a rape case in Upper Moreland. Daniel admitted to using methamphetamines in 1984. He also stated he had witnessed George's daily use of meth and his selling it to others (including Daniel). Daniel could not remember George's red LeMans, despite being given a detailed description of the car's exterior and interior design. Interestingly, he denied ever witnessing violent or aggressive behavior from George with anyone while he was high on meth. He stated he did not hang out with George for long periods of time in those days.

While George was living in Bensalem, Daniel and George barely spoke to one another. He knew very well of the Sanders brothers and described them as "trouble" and "con artists." Interestingly, he remembered Gary Burros but didn't remember Kim Sullivan, Mark Litman, or Robert Romanski. He and Burros used to hang out, and Daniel said he was also a "meth guy," but denied ever hanging out with the crowd at the McDonald's in Hatboro with the rest of the "meth gang."

Daniel's wife Ellen said that when they married in May of 1984, Daniel was cleaning up his act and "was not allowed to hang out" with that crowd. She also commented that Lori was "not a nice person" and that she could be "pretty nasty," which kept them from spending time together.

CHAPTER 16
Going To Trial

After almost two years of pre-trial motions and postponements, George Shaw went on trial in July 2017. Surprisingly, he elected to have a waiver trial instead of a jury trial. This means that the case would only be heard by the judge and the verdict would be decided by the judge. In other words, there would be no jury. Shaw's mother borrowed against her mortgage to pay for two of the best attorneys in Bucks County so he wouldn't have to settle for a public defender.

Robert Rowan's testimony was heart-wrenching and excellent. He attested to knocking on the door of the red house the night Barbara went missing. He stated that a male had answered the door the night of August 3, 1984, and told him Barbara wasn't there, which correlates with Sanders' statement. At one point, Mr. Rowan was asked if his memory of events was accurate, and he replied, "How could I forget?"

Robert Sanders repeated his grand jury testimony and told the court what he witnessed on the evening of August 3, 1984. His testimony was damaging to the defense. He recounted helping Shaw dispose of Barbara Rowan's body after seeing her lying lifeless on Shaw's bed. The defense attacked his credibility during cross-examination, but his testimony was solid. One unique aspect of Sanders was that when he testified truthfully to the investigating grand jury, he had not yet been charged with any crimes. As much as the defense wanted to accuse him of lying to work off charges, the argument wasn't applicable; he was not a witness corrupted by making a deal on his own charges. Sanders was not charged until after his testimony to the investigating grand jury. Despite being three decades late, his honesty also resulted in his arrest.

"Crimes conceived in hell don't have angels as witnesses" is a quote often used in criminal law. To prosecute criminals, district attorneys often must use witnesses who are "less than angels" to testify against them. Jennifer applied this quote to Sanders during her closing argument to the court. Sanders was no angel; he had kept the truth about the night Barbara was killed from police for over 30 years. That said, he was not like Shaw, who was a rapist, given the home invasion incident he committed in Montgomery County. Sanders was never arrested for crimes against people. He had numerous DUI, public drunkenness, and drug charges, and a burglary at a Dairy Queen, which made him a felon, but he had never been arrested for rape, assault, or anything violent. I've often speculated that Sanders self-medicated so much his entire adult life because he was keeping this dark secret about Shaw killing Barbara.

Danny Green testified to what he and his wife had witnessed on the side of the road on the evening of August 3, 1984. He spoke of the car that matched the description of Shaw's missing Pontiac LeMans that had disappeared. He testified that he and his wife observed two men who looked like Shaw and Sanders—one wearing a painter's cap style hat, the other with dark hair and dark-rimmed glasses—standing by the open trunk at the very location where Barbara's body was found thirteen days later.

Another witness, Timmy Johnson, testified that on August 3—the day Barbara went missing—he had knocked on the door of Shaw's neighbor to inquire about a car they had for sale. Nobody answered, and while he was there, a young girl with long red hair matching Barbara's description opened Shaw's door from inside the apartment with an adult white male, matching Shaw's description, behind her. They both told him that the neighbors were not home. More importantly, Johnson saw Barbara at the Shaw residence during the time she was unaccounted for.

Assistant District Attorney Jess Bryant had been assigned as second chair on the case. She was tasked with compiling information on tape manufacturing and securing expert testimony from the FBI analyst—a task she handled perfectly. The forensic scientist from the FBI Laboratory who examined and compared the tape found on Barbara's body to the rolls of tape found in

Shaw's possession gave damaging testimony under direct examination by Bryant. The tape from Barbara's body was identical in filament and fibers to the tape found in Shaw's possession, and they originated from the same source. The tape was identical and not available to the general public.

Dan Colacicco testified that he worked at M&C Specialties, where the tape was manufactured, and that he had given several rolls of the tape to Shaw a few months before he moved to his apartment in Trevose in 1984.

Detective Mosiniak, I, and other active and retired law enforcement gave testimony one by one as to our roles in the investigation. A forensic pathologist who reviewed the notes from the original autopsy testified and concurred with the manner and cause of death being homicide by asphyxiation.

Witness after witness, the prosecution presented the case to the court to prove Shaw guilty.

Patricia Rowan was not called to testify at the criminal trial, but she did write a heart-rending impact statement. In the document, she pleaded with Judge Wallace Bateman to serve justice and put Shaw away in prison. She stated how she only had fourteen years with Barbara while Shaw had remained surrounded by his family for the last thirty-one years. He stole that away from her, Mrs. Rowan said. She even stopped going to birthday parties and baby showers because it was too hurtful. "I will never know what it feels like to watch Barbara grow up and become something—a mother; or be able to know what it's like to become a grandmother," Patricia Rowan described with despair.

On July 31, 2017, George Franz Shaw was found guilty of third-degree murder and attempted sexual assault. He escaped first- and second-degree murder because the judge didn't believe the prosecution had proved it. First-degree murder constitutes a specific intent to kill; second-degree murder is a homicide that occurs during the commission of another felony, such as robbery or rape. Shaw had to be sentenced according to third-degree murder statutes as they were in 1984. Back then, it was ten to twenty years; now, it's twenty to forty years. We couldn't get a conviction for rape because there was never any semen recovered at the scene, and DNA testing was non-existent then. However, we did convict him for attempted sexual assault since she was found with her hands and feet bound and undressed from the waist down.

Shaw was sentenced to thirteen to twenty-nine years for third-degree murder and sexual assault.

To say I was disappointed over this sentencing would be an understatement. There is no question that this murder occurred during the commission of another felony: rape. However, since we couldn't prove rape, we lost second-degree murder. Shaw is serving his sentence in Rockview State Prison located in Center County, Pennsylvania, and he'll do the max because of the circumstances, but it is still not enough.

Although I reopened this case in 2002, Shaw wasn't convicted until July 2017—thirty-three years after Barbara's murder.

The sentencing of Robert Sanders took place after Shaw's trial. He received a sentence of three to seven years on charges of "preventing the apprehension of a felon."

But Barbara's chapter didn't end there for me. On February 21, 2018 (post-trial), I felt like an idiot sitting in a New York City television studio in front of renowned journalist and news anchor Paula Zahn. I found myself crying like a seven-year-old boy who had just watched the end of *Old Yeller*. I cried my eyes out when I saw that stupid movie, and to this day, I hate it. It reminds me too much of my beloved childhood dog, Smokey.

Anyway, on the TV set of *On the Case with Paula Zahn*, there was a crew of strangers pointing lights and cameras at me at a time when I'd never felt more vulnerable in my entire life. At that point, I realized that I had internalized a lot of emotions over the fifteen years of working on the Rowan case. Paula Zahn managed to open the floodgates without breaking a sweat. She's a hell of an interviewer; I'll give her that. I thought of how close I was to this case as a fourteen-year-old kid and why I had been so determined to solve it. I thought about Barbara and her family, all they had lost and endured for decades, and how this would honor what they had gone through. Sadly, both original lead detectives, Dave Rouland and Bill Koszarek, had passed away within weeks of the show's production. They would never see this on television, which bothered me. They were supposed to do the show with us.

Down the hall in the holding room was Heather, now my wife, best friend, and the love of my life. My longtime friend and partner on the case Mike Mosiniak was also there, along with my friend Jennifer Schorn and her second chair on the case, Jessica Bryant. The case would never have been solved had it not been for them. Also at the studio were Denice and Jackie, Barbara's cousins, who never missed a day in court. After filming, I had to walk back into the holding room and try to make it look as though I hadn't lost it.

On a more positive note, former KYW3 TV news reporter Frank Traynor covered the Barbara Rowan story in 1984 and, fortunately, was able to be part of the Paula Zahn experience. He even provided some of the original news footage to use on the show. The episode aired on the Investigation Discovery channel on July 29, 2018. Although Traynor and I both had ties to the Barbara Rowan case, we never realized it until one day in 2012 when we took the train home after a SAG-AFTRA meeting. Back then, both he and I served as board members for the SAG-AFTRA union in Philadelphia.

That day, we began chatting, and he asked, "You work in Bensalem?" I answered, "Yes." He said, "I recall covering a story about a young girl who was murdered in the early '80s up there." I replied, "Are you joking with me?" He answered, "No." I told him I'd been working on that case for ten years—the Rowan case. He said, "Yes, that's the name: Barbara Rowan." It took another six years down the pike, but we finally solved it.

After that, I wanted to carry Frank Friel's legacy and solve the Publicker Jane Doe case. But I needed additional resources. I'd first learned of the Vidocq Society when I walked into Frank's office and asked about the sculpture of Publicker Jane Doe. I was intrigued by the Vidocq Society—a vast room full of the most elite in their profession working together to solve unsolved homicide cases.

Jim "Fitz" Fitzgerald was a Bensalem Police officer before he became an FBI agent. He is a friend of mine and a Vidocq Society member. Fitz is well-known for his involvement in the Unabomber investigation, resulting in the arrest and conviction of Ted Kaczynski. The Netflix mini-series *Manhunt* depicts the details of his involvement in the investigation. One day, Fitz invited me to a Vidocq Society meeting as his guest and later sponsored me for membership in 2017.

The Vidocq Society is a non-profit, worldly crime-fighting club that was founded about thirty years ago by three reputable professionals: Richard Walters (criminal psychiatrist), Frank Bender (forensic artist/sculptor), and William Fleischer (retired Customs agent and now Vidocq Society commissioner emeritus). The Vidocq Society was named after Eugene Francois Vidocq, a French criminal-turned-detective. He helped police by using his knowledge from a criminal's perspective to solve cold case murders. Vidocq is considered "the father of modern forensics." *The Murder Room* is a book by Michael Capuzzo about the Vidocq Society in 2010. It goes back to the very beginning as to how it was founded, and there is even a mention of Publicker Jane Doe in the book, since Bender was professionally involved in her investigation.

The Vidocq Society holds monthly luncheons at the Union League of Philadelphia. The room is filled with anywhere from fifty to eighty professionals, including retired homicide investigators, FBI profilers, criminal psychologists, medical pathologists, doctors… everyone from various backgrounds. Collectively, they use their professional knowledge and experience to offer new and untried avenues of investigation for cases gone cold. During these meetings, the room transforms into a giant think tank. Each month, a new cold case is chosen, and a PowerPoint is presented to the members. It's compelling to watch everyone brainstorm and ask questions about things that may or may not have already been done on the case.

The Vidocq Society has dedicated itself to several cases, including one of the longest-standing unsolved cold cases in the country known as "The Boy in the Box," otherwise named "America's Lost Child." It remained unsolved for more than sixty years. A little boy was found dead inside a cardboard box in the Fox Chase section of Philadelphia on February 25, 1957. The unidentified boy, believed to be between the ages of four and six, was naked and badly beaten. His hair had been freshly cut, which appeared to have been done in a hurry or fit of rage because of bald spots from the razor. The cause of death was determined to be head trauma. He had several scars, including one on his chin, but oddly no evidence of broken bones.

I had the honor of spending some time with the original investigator of this case, Detective Bill Kelly. My mother used to work as a receptionist at an assisted living facility in the Fox Chase section of Northeast Philadelphia. Kelly lived there, and through small talk between him and my mother, she told him what I did for a living. He asked if I would come by sometime and meet him, and I finally did in early 2012. Kelly and I had coffee and spent a few hours together.

He told me about the case and how he had bought clothes to dress the boy in and sat him up for photos, hoping that someone would recognize him if the boy appeared more natural/alive. But all possible leads went cold. Kelly even gave me one of the original flyers with the photos he took of the boy that was distributed in the *Philadelphia Bulletin* in 1957; he even signed it. (Insert photo if wanted)

The Vidocq Society adopted this case, and several years ago, a small monument was erected near the site where his body was found. In 1998, a segment about "The Boy in the Box" aired on *America's Most Wanted*, leading to a resurgence of the case. Although I had never personally worked on this case, the Vidocq Society committed themselves to solving it and put up the finances to have his remains exhumed for DNA genealogy. The unidentified boy's remains were sent to a lab overseas, and genealogists worked tirelessly alongside detectives to make great strides in the investigation. On December 8, 2022, the boy was finally identified as Joseph Augustus Zarelli. He was only four years old when he died.

Although the boy has now been identified, the investigation remains active and ongoing in hopes of making an arrest for the child's death. However, given the amount of years that have passed since his death, his killer, or killers, are most likely deceased.

Joseph's body was initially buried at the Dunksferry Road potter's field until the Vidocq Society paid to have his body moved to the Ivy Hill Cemetery in 1998. "America's Unknown Child" marked his gravestone, and the Vidocq Society hosted an annual memorial service. The headstone has since been changed and now displays his given name.

The Dunksferry Road potter's field is also known as Philadelphia's last potter's field, where hundreds of unclaimed and unidentified people are buried. The field opened in 1956, and the land stretches about 500 feet deep and 200 feet wide. Cement blocks with grave numbers mark each of the unclaimed persons. Unfortunately, the markers are no longer visible as the cemetery is poorly maintained.

Potter's field is a biblical term that originates from the story of Judas. After he hanged himself, the priests who paid him to betray Jesus used his thirty silver pieces to purchase a plot of ground for his burial. The field had been where potters mined clay for their work, so the land was not ideal for agriculture. The term has become the catchword for all public burial grounds where the poor and unidentified are laid to rest.

The first potter's field in Philadelphia, Dunksferry Potter's Field, was established at Washington Square in 1705. Numerous other potter's fields were spread around the city but were eventually built over by shameless developers. It is estimated that there was an average of one hundred unclaimed bodies buried in that first potter's field yearly. Dunksferry was decommissioned in 1987, due to lack of space, according to officials. More recently, locals have reported kids riding ATVs on the far side of the Dunksferry grounds, and it has become a party hangout for teens where crushed beer cans and empty liquor bottles litter the property. Now, where the boy's headstone used to be lies lumpy mounds of groundhog-disturbed earth.

CHAPTER 17
Publicker Jane Doe

I was determined to finish Frank Friel's work on Publicker Jane Doe, and I didn't want to accept that a young girl could be dead, missing, and unidentified for so long. As far as I was concerned, she deserved as much attention as "The Boy in the Box." All unidentified victims deserve to be identified.

Her remains laid there for several years before discovery. Some clothes, jewelry, and black stockings were found nearby. No missing person reports were linked to her. I have worked on her case since 2004—approximately seventeen years. I thought, "Someone's got to be missing her." I didn't want her to be forgotten.

In the early 1900s, the Publicker Distillery had two large plants in Pennsylvania, one in South Philadelphia and the other in Bensalem.

At the time, the distilleries were primarily known for manufacturing and selling industrial alcohol solvents for

Publicker Industries Plant, 1947
Credit: George D. McDowell, Philadelphia; Evening
Bulletin Collection, Special Collections Research
Center, Temple

cleaning supplies, otherwise known as ethanol. But in the 1950s, after Prohibition, they began to make whiskey, which proved to be a successful and productive business move. However, a change of ownership and some fatal explosions eventually led to the demise of both Publicker Distilleries in the late 1980s. The buildings were torn down and abandoned, becoming hangouts for teens to party and a playground for criminal activity.

One afternoon in January 1988, a couple was walking their dog on the abandoned property of the once-standing Publicker Distillery. Although the main building had been torn down, two or three old underground pump houses and smaller buildings still existed. They looked similar to wells from the outside, with a big cement bulkhead sticking out of the ground and a steel ladder to climb down into it.

Present day photo - the underground pump house where Publicker Jane Doe's remains were discovered Credit: Bensalem PD

You could see the big wheels, valves, and pipes used for something in the function of the distillery at one point. The couple looked down one of those wells and saw what they initially thought was a mannequin lying across a colossal pipe. But when they looked closer, they realized it was a human skeleton and immediately called the police.

She was young, estimated to be anywhere from seventeen to twenty-one years old. A white female, petite, with an approximate weight of 120 pounds. She had long brown hair that they could describe because they found her with a little bit of hair still left on her skull. But the most interesting thing about her was that she was pregnant, evident by the fetal bones found within her. There were no signs of blunt force trauma or fractures to her skull that would have led to an apparent cause of death, although she did have a minor fracture on her right maxilla (jawbone). There was nothing to indicate that she had been shot or stabbed. She was dressed, and there were no signs of sexual assault that could be determined.

She wore Braxton designer jeans and a purple, fancy, mesh-like top. There were two to three pairs of shoes near her body and a couple of black nylon stockings—as if there may have been a duffel bag that belonged to her, and the contents were dumped alongside her.

Investigators tried to identify her but had no luck— DNA was in its early stages in the late 1980s. Years later, Frank Friel reached out to renowned forensic artist Frank Bender, one of the founders of the Vidocq Society. He was famous for his accuracy in sculpting the faces of unidentified remains. He recreated Jane Doe's face but, unfortunately, the photo did not generate any leads. Whatever leads detectives thought they had led to nothing, and her remains were placed into storage with the label "Publicker Jane Doe."

In 2004, under George W. Bush's presidency, a new order was signed for a program called "The President's DNA Initiative," which fell under the Justice for All Act.

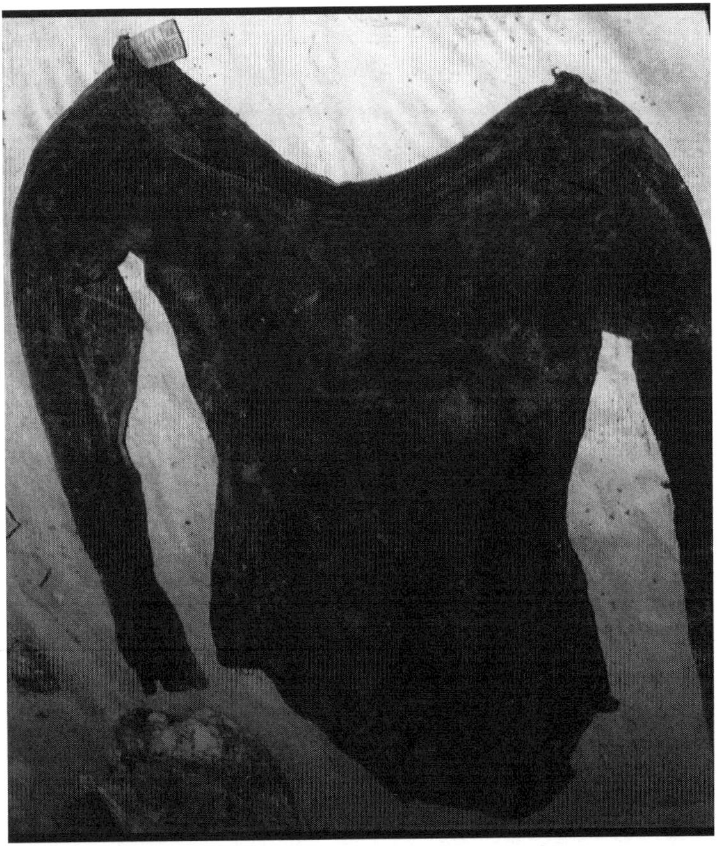

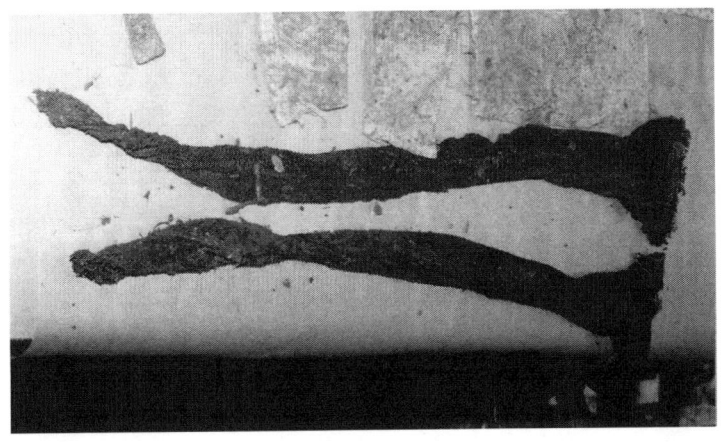

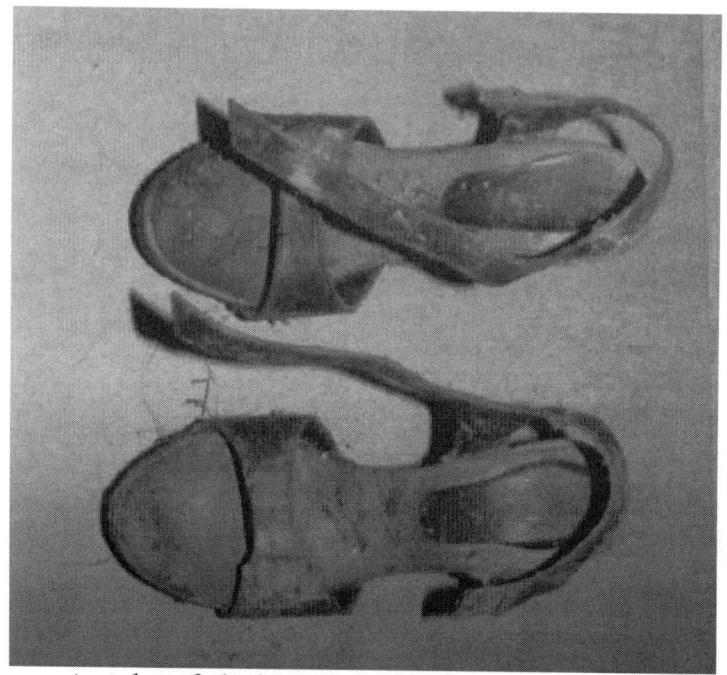

**Articles of clothing found with the remains of
Publicker Jane Doe in 1988
Credit: Bensalem PD**

It was to provide funding for DNA collection and analysis efforts for all Jane and John Does throughout the country. I took advantage of that by sending her bones, which had still been in evidence, to "The Center for Human Identification" at the University of North Texas. At no cost to us, they extracted her DNA profile and uploaded it into the FBI's CODIS (Combined DNA Index System), the national database for DNA profiles for missing persons, unidentified persons, or those suspected or even convicted of a crime.

CODIS is a software platform that blends forensic science and computer technology. Analysts use CODIS to search DNA profiles retrieved from crime scene evidence against DNA profiles from other crime scenes and convicted offenders and arrestees. Put simply, for missing persons and John and Jane Does, it can compare DNA profiles and identify Does as missing persons through family reference samples of DNA.

I was happy about getting Publicker Jane Doe into CODIS, knowing if another agency put in a family reference sample of somebody missing a family member, we could get a DNA match and identify Publicker Jane Doe.

DNA testing was done on the fetal bones, which determined the baby was a female. It was not a full profile but still suitable for comparison testing. In other words, although the profile was incomplete, it could be compared to a specific profile if a potential father was suspected. One theory at this point was that whoever killed Publicker Jane Doe may have been the baby's father. If we ever identified her, we could follow the victimology of who she was and what was going on in her life then and possibly be able to find her killer too.

Returning to the original files from the 1980s, I tracked down all the leads I could to see if something was missed or overlooked. During that process, I stumbled upon the case of Jeannette Tambe. Jeanette was twenty-one when she went missing from her Bensalem home in 1984. A close family friend and neighbor, Joanne Fox, contacted the police after seeing a photo of Publicker Jane Doe's composite on the news. She thought it looked a lot like Jeanette. Bender also believed Jeanette was my Publicker Jane Doe, so I focused on Jeanette. But, as it turned out, Bender's theory was wrong.

Jeanette's parents were deceased when I came into the picture in 2009. She had one surviving brother, Joseph Tambe, who I had a great deal of trouble tracking down. With the help of the FBI, we were able to locate him in Nanticoke, Pennsylvania, outside of Scranton.

In the fall of 2009, I drove to Joseph Tambe's home and visited with him. He could not identify any of Publicker Jane Doe's clothing or jewelry. He explained that when Jeanette disappeared, the family figured she had run off with her boyfriend and would return any day, but she never did.

Joseph consented to give me a DNA sample, so I collected some buccal (mouth) swabs for saliva and sent them to the Center for Human Identification. They could extract his DNA from the swabs and upload it into CODIS. I was confident I would get a hit between him and Publicker Jane Doe.

Several months later, I arrived at work for the day shift and noticed a letter from the University of North Texas on my desk. I opened it, and the letter informed me there had been an association made with Joseph Tambe's DNA. Coincidentally, at the same time, my phone was ringing, so I took the call, and it was also the University of North Texas. They told me that Joseph's DNA sample had a "Mitochondrial DNA" match, which identifies sibling matches. But his sibling's DNA match was with a different Jane Doe found in Buena Vista, New Jersey, in 1986—not my Publicker Jane Doe. I was confused by this, but I followed the lead.

The medical examiner in New Jersey refused to identify Buena Vista Jane Doe as Jeanette Tambe because we did not have a "nuclear DNA" match, which is a DNA match with her parents. So we needed nuclear DNA that we could only get from her deceased parents. This was a problem, and there was no budget for an exhumation. I contacted Joseph again, and he informed me that his parents had been cremated, so that idea's fate was sealed.

From there, I contacted Detective Lachman, the original investigator on the Tambe case. He had since retired from the Bensalem PD and was working for the district attorney. I explained everything to him about finding Jeanette Tambe and how we needed nuclear DNA to declare Buena Vista Jane Doe as Jeanette Tambe. He calmly asked, "Why don't you just give them her mom's blood to test?" We were on the phone then, but if he could have seen my face, I'm sure it would have made him laugh. I had no clue about the existence of any blood. I asked, "What blood from her mom?" He told me that somewhere around 1985, he had taken two vials of blood from Jeanette's mother, Joy Tambe, in case it was ever needed for identification purposes. There was no record of the blood being collected in the dusty and worn case file. Luckily, Detective Lachman had a copy of the file and agreed to meet me the next day at the Bensalem PD.

The following morning, Detective Lachman arrived and handed me a property receipt I had never seen before. No copy of this property receipt was in my case file. It listed two vials of blood taken from Joy Tambe in early 1985 that were placed into evidence.

Almost twenty-five years had passed since this blood was collected, and our agency was working out of a different building in 1985. I admit, I didn't have high hopes that the blood was still in our possession. Once we arrived at the evidence room, I handed the receipt to the evidence custodian, Bill Thompson. He looked at the paperwork and smirked. I said, "I know, it's from 1985, but can you just check, please?"

Come to find out, he laughed because he knew exactly where the two vials of blood were. I was shocked we still had the blood. Bill got them for us, and I immediately contacted the New Jersey State Police (NJSP) and told them we had blood from Jeanette Tambe's mother. We took it to the NJSP lab that day, and the results came a week later. We had a nuclear DNA match between the blood from Joy Tambe and Buena Vista Jane Doe. She was officially Jeanette Tambe.

Whoever had killed her had done it out of sheer cruelty. Her body had numerous superficial stab wounds, and her hands and feet were bound. Sulfuric acid was poured on her face, chest, and throat, possibly to prevent identification. The medical examiner ruled her manner and cause of death homicide by asphyxiation. The NJSP has jurisdiction over the homicide, and a suspect has been developed.

A second theory on the identity of Publicker Jane Doe led me to the case of a fourteen-year-old Bensalem girl named Tracy Byrd. A long-term case manager from the National Center for Missing and Exploited Children (NCMEC) contacted me. They wanted to follow up on Tracy's case, but the original investigators had retired. Tracy Byrd had disappeared in the spring of 1983 after her mother's boyfriend, Paul Greenwald, allegedly dropped her off at school. However, according to school records, she never attended school that day and was marked absent.

Records indicated that Tracy had been suspended from school, but she didn't tell her mom, so she continued to act as if she was going to school while she was cutting class. Rumors also went public about her possibly being pregnant and running away. The case received much media attention then, and her mother, Jean Byrd, pleaded for Tracy's return home. But about seven months later, in the fall of 1983, Tracy's mother, Jean, also went missing. A few weeks after her disappearance, Jean's body was found lying in a shallow grave in Black Bird State Forest located in Delaware. She had been murdered.

The Delaware State Police led the investigation, and ultimately, Paul Greenwald was arrested for Jean's murder. It is unclear to me if he ever made it to trial or was in prison awaiting trial, but while in prison, he committed suicide. Greenwald was interviewed by both the Delaware State Police and the Bensalem Police in connection to Tracy's disappearance. Although he was the last person to see Tracy alive, he denied any involvement with Tracy's disappearance or having any knowledge of where she was or what her fate was. If he was involved in Tracy's disappearance, he took it to the grave.

There were a lot of commonalities between Tracy and Publicker Jane Doe. The Publicker Distillery was less than two miles from where Tracy lived, and it was a well-known place for teens to hang out. But it was also the ideal place for a murderer to hide a dead body. Anthropologists estimated that Publicker Jane Doe's body had been there anywhere from three to five years, so the time frame was accurate.

There were also many common physical characteristics between Tracy and Publicker Jane Doe. They were both petite and of similar height—around five feet, one inch tall. Their hair color and length were alike. And speculations that Tracy had been pregnant correlated with the fetal bones found in Jane Doe's remains. But I needed DNA to move forward with this investigation. Tracy's mother was dead and had been cremated, so retrieving DNA from her remains was not an option.

Tracy had two half-brothers who still lived in Philadelphia, so I contacted them. Their father was also still alive in New Jersey, and I met with all three of them and explained why I was there. Before I took the father's buccal swab, he revealed that he was not sure he was Tracy's father. I collected the swab anyway on the chance that he may have been her father.

Shortly after, I met Jean's mother—Tracy's maternal grandmother—and collected a DNA swab from her. All four family reference samples were sent to the University of North Texas and CODIS. However, none of them rendered an association with Publicker Jane Doe.

I was desperate for some answers, but without her mother being alive or knowing who Tracy's father was, I had to come to terms with this and accept the facts. If I at least had Jean's DNA to put into CODIS and still did not get any hits, I would be satisfied that Publicker Jane Doe was not Tracy.

But Tracy has not been forgotten. It was a known fact that Greenwald frequently camped at Black Bird State Forest in Delaware. Since Jean's body was found there, searching for Tracy's remains there is also worth a shot. With generous help from the National Center for Missing and Exploited Children (NCMEC), plans for executing a search in Black Bird State Forest are being made. Specific areas of the park will be searched with cadaver dogs. This project will include Delaware state troopers, members of NCMEC, Bensalem Police, and park rangers. Recently, NCMEC began to use a technique called LiDAR, which can be used to find graves of unmarked decedents. It detects an elevation change in the ground where the bodies are buried. Unfortunately, the search was postponed due to COVID-19 pandemic restrictions, but plans are in place to proceed.

In 2013, I was contacted by a woman named Cathy DeBuono. DeBuono is from Los Angeles and had a theory that Publicker Jane Doe may have been a victim of Victor Lawrence Paleologus. Paleologus was infamous for reeling in actresses and models by pretending to be a casting director and luring them to a remote spot for so-called "photo shoots." He would tell them to bring extra sets of clothing with them so they would have multiple outfits to wear for the photos. Once at the isolated locations, Paleologus would sexually assault the women. DeBuono was concerned there were more victims.

DeBuono is an actress known for playing the role of M'Pella on *Star Trek: Deep Space Nine*, among other roles. She was among the numerous victims targeted by Paleologos, but fortunately, she got away. Kristi Johnson was murdered by Paleologus in Los Angeles in 2003, and DeBuono and other survivors testified against him at his murder trial as to his manipulative and deceitful tactics. DeBuono had researched and discovered that he had lived in Bensalem in 1985. This put him there around the estimated time of Publicker Jane Doe's death.

The fact that Publicker Jane Doe was found in an isolated area with multiple articles of clothing and more than one pair of shoes suggested a similarity to her and the previous victims of Paleologus. Additionally, Paleologus had a residence and relatives in Bensalem in 1985 which put him in the area a few years before Publicker Jane Doe's death. All of this was circumstantial, but it did get my attention and I began to wonder if Publicker Jane Doe had been a victim of Victor Paleologus.

Yolanda McClary, former Las Vegas CSI (Crime Scene Investigator), is a forensic specialist who is widely known for her skill in recovering DNA. She retired from the Las Vegas Police Department after twenty-six years of service and was featured on the popular TNT series *Cold Justice*. McClary also inspired Marg Helgenberger's character Catherine Willows on the TV show *CSI: Crime Scene Investigation*. The once-popular crime series aired on TV from 2000 to 2015 and returned in 2021. McClary's latest television series, *The Jane Doe Murders*, aired its first Oxygen Network episode on January 3, 2021.

McClary first contacted me on April 24, 2019. By this time, I had already posted our Publicker Jane Doe on the National Missing and Unidentified Persons System (NamUs) just to get the information out there. There were published photographs of her clothing and jewelry, along with forensic sculptures of her skull. This is where McClary first found the information on Publicker Jane Doe and took a genuine interest in the case.

McClary and her producer asked me to appear on an episode of *The Jane Doe Murders*. I was on board, but then the COVID-19 pandemic hit, and TV production came to a screeching halt. We remained in touch, and in December 2020 McClary and I began to plug away on the Publicker Jane Doe case.

Although Publicker Jane Doe's DNA profile was in CODIS, we needed to extract her profile again to attempt Investigative genetic genealogy (IGG). The DNA testing previously done for CODIS was not suitable for genealogy databases. BODE Technologies was the lab where Publicker Jane Doe's bones were sent. They drilled the bones to extract her DNA and, with the help of Othram Labs, subsequently produced a DNA profile. When these profiles are completed, they contain numbers that are then uploaded into open-source databases. Open-source databases are separate from private ones like Ancestry.com. Private databases do not even accept profile uploads. When profiles are uploaded to open-source databases, they generally list the top matches first. Then it usually takes months to build a family tree. When BODE Technologies initially uploaded the profile, the matches were very distant and somewhat despairing for the case. At best, they had possibly associated a fourth and fifth cousin. BODE recommended leaving the profile where it was and seeing if more associations came in down the line. That is when I turned things over to McClary.

Finally, a significant break occurred in the Publicker Jane Doe case. About a year passed, and no more genealogical associations had been made with Publicker Jane Doe. GEDmatch is a free, non-profit DNA website constructed for genealogy research. Unlike sites like AncestryDNA and 23andMe, GEDmatch allows users to upload their raw data into the platform. But McClary learned GEDmatch had since changed ownership. This resulted in the creation of some new algorithms. On a hunch, McClary entered the Publicker Jane Doe profile into GEDmatch a second time. This time, "it produced a hit to one excellent match and two others that were a bit more distant," McClary shared in a KYW Newsradio podcast.

Back in the fall of 2020, I was contacted by Tom Rickert and Kristen Johanson of the popular KYW true crime podcast *Gone Cold*. They wanted to do a podcast series with me about Publicker Jane Doe. Four episodes later, the investigation unfolded right before our very eyes.

Now there were various DNA associations between the genealogy of Publicker Jane Doe and several identified relatives from Philadelphia and elsewhere in Pennsylvania. Everything was moving at a swift pace and in the right direction. McClary and her partner genealogist built the family tree and identified Publicker Jane Doe in under four days.

On January 15, 2021, I received a phone call from McClary late in the afternoon, informing me that she had found two matched siblings. She said with as much confidence as I've ever heard anyone make a statement, "I found Linda and Joseph Todd. Your Jane Doe is their sister."

But it wasn't over yet. Now I was faced with tracking Jane Doe's siblings down and finding phone numbers to contact them. I did my own research, and when looking into name databases, I discovered that Joseph Todd had a daughter with a working phone number and an email address. I called and left a message for her, and she called me back within a few minutes. She was very cooperative when I asked if she knew of her father once having a sister who went missing. She replied, "Yes, in 1985, his sister disappeared." The next question I asked was his sister's name, and she answered, "Lisa." I told her that I believed

I had found Lisa and asked her to have her father call me. I slammed my fist on the desk the second I hung up the phone. "We got her; we got her!" One of the nearby officers looked over and asked what was going on. I explained that I had finally identified my Jane Doe.

An emotional Joseph called me within the hour, and we spoke about his missing sister. I then immediately drove to his home in Philadelphia with Sergeant Adam Kolman and Detective Neil Tropiano. He confirmed his sister's information and identified photos of the two rings found with Lisa's body. Joseph was Lisa's younger brother and was only thirteen when she went missing. He told us his parents had reported her missing to the Philadelphia Police. Sadly, both of their parents had passed away a couple of years prior, not ever knowing what happened to their daughter. Buccal swabs were collected from him and his sister Linda, allowing us to compare Publicker Jane Doe's DNA to theirs. The result was that they were first-degree relatives. Publicker Jane Doe now had her name; she was officially Lisa Todd.

Joseph and Linda said they knew she was pregnant when she disappeared. Linda was about ten or eleven when she last remembered seeing Lisa. "We just thought Lisa ran away," Linda stated. Over the years, Linda made numerous attempts to locate her sister, calling several prisons to see if she could be in jail. That would be a valid reason to prevent Lisa's return home. While Linda was thankful for the information, she communicated a strong understanding that finding her sister's killer would not bring Lisa back.

With the help of the Bensalem Police Department, BODE Technology Group, Othram Labs, and Yolanda McClary, Publicker Jane Doe was finally identified and publicly revealed as Lisa Todd during a local news press conference on March 3, 2021.

We also learned that Lisa had a two-year-old son in 1985. Today, he is in his mid-thirties, and I've had the privilege to meet him. Out of respect for his privacy, I will not reveal his name, but he was very appreciative of the information we gave him. Through all the years, he thought his mother had abandoned him. But now he knew the truth.

I won't pull punches for the Lisa Todd case. She was seventeen years old when she disappeared but had been removed from the missing persons' database shortly after her eighteenth birthday, yet she was still missing. I was never able to get an explanation from the Philadelphia PD as to why she was removed, nor were they ever able to produce a missing person report, despite our requests. This bothers me; people don't just stop being missing after their eighteenth birthday. They failed Lisa, her family, and society. Had she been left in the system; she likely would have been identified quickly after her body's discovery. Instead, she remained a Jane Doe in our evidence room for thirty-three years. This is a sore spot for me, and I want to call out the system failures because God only knows how many other missing/deceased kids were removed from the system (National Crime Information Center) after their eighteenth birthday. In the end, I would like to give credit to the National Center for Missing & Exploited Children, who discovered Lisa Todd was, in fact, reported missing in October 1985 after searching her name in purged records.

Over the years, there have been various sketches and three-dimensional computer-generated recreations of Publicker Jane Doe. After identifying Lisa, the family kindly provided me with photos of Lisa and her young son before she went missing. Frank Bender's sculpture is by far the closest to her look in life.

Frank Bender's Reconstruction of Publicker Jane Doe
Credit: Chris McMullin

I mentioned earlier that in the book *The Murder Room*, a section mentions the Publicker Jane Doe case. It reads: "Frank Bender was furious with cops and expressed frustration with officers who gave up on cases he was still dedicated to, 'such as the skeletal remains of the young woman and her unborn fetus, also known as Publicker Jane Doe.'" I am curious as to why Bender believed officers gave up on the case—I knew both original investigators, and they did everything they could. Unfortunately, Bender was no longer with us to ask that question. He passed away in 2011, shortly after the release of *The Murder Room*, and I'm grateful to have had the chance to spend the time I did with him thirteen years ago.

On another meaningful note, I was honored to have been invited to Lisa's memorial service. I removed her jewelry from the evidence room and gave it to her son. I know the memories she left behind will be in better hands with him rather than sitting in an evidence box. He expressed peace with the investigation despite not yet finding the person responsible for his mother's death. He now knows she didn't abandon him and has some closure.

CHAPTER 18
Club House Jane Doe

In August 1995, some children played in a wooded lot behind the Club House Diner on Street Road in Bensalem, Pennsylvania. They saw what they thought was a turtle shell sticking out of the ground. Instead, it turned out to be a human skull. Police were called, and an entire human skeleton was unveiled from a shallow grave. She earned the name "Club House Jane Doe," and an autopsy report approximated her remains as those of an adult female in her mid-thirties. The forensic pathologist classified the death a "homicide by asphyxiation" and estimated the remains had been behind the Club House Diner for about three years, placing her last alive in 1992. She had given birth at least once and had extensive low-grade dental work (possibly done at a clinic or in prison). Items found with her remains included a KPMG Peat Marwick shirt, another shirt that read "Property of Alcatraz Penitentiary Swim Team," and two crucifixes—one gold and one silver—that depicted the stations of the cross.

I began working on this case in 2002 and discovered that, in 1993, William Montgomery of Bensalem had been arrested for the deaths of two exotic dancers in 1992 and 1993. He pleaded guilty to avoid the death penalty. Their bodies were found only a few miles away from one another, and Montgomery himself lived about a mile from the Club House Diner. Investigators believed there were more victims out there but could never successfully connect any other deaths to him. Montgomery is currently serving a double life sentence for the murders he committed, which happened around the same timeframe as the Club House Jane Doe was believed to have been killed. Club House Jane Doe's body was wrapped in plastic, as were those of the other two women he murdered.

Many people theorize that Montgomery is responsible for the murder of Club House Jane Doe. Although he has never been charged for it, the theory is circumstantial. In 2004, I persuaded the district attorney and my department to exhume Club House Jane Doe's body because more grant money was available for DNA testing. If I could get her exhumed, I could have her DNA profile extracted and uploaded into the CODIS system.

This was a huge opportunity because I had a chance to begin using current investigative technology on this case. All cold case investigations need to be brought up to current standards if they're to be solved. The Doe Network is a 100% volunteer non-profit organization that helps with missing persons and Doe cases. It provided the services of a forensic artist and sculptor at no cost. With the help of The Doe Network, we could get an image of what she looked like in life. Daniel Sollitti, deputy chief of police in Jersey City, New Jersey, and FBI-trained forensic artist, completed a sketch. Also, forensic artist Seth Wolfson created a three-dimensional sculpture of the victim's face. This reminded me of the time in 1994 when Frank Friel showed me the sculpture of Publicker Jane Doe made by Frank Bender.

As of January 2021, the CODIS system had eliminated close to forty missing women as being the Club House Diner Jane Doe. We hoped we could identify Club House Jane Doe the same way we identified Lisa Todd. At my request, Director Harran approved DNA testing for genetic genealogy, and once again, BODE did the lab work on Club House Jane Doe. We were trying to catch lightning twice and identify our other Doe.

Months later, after the genetic profile was obtained and uploaded, we again had some distant matches, but no close associations had been made.

The night before our monthly Vidocq Society meeting in late November 2021, several of us met for dinner, including a friend of mine, Jennifer Moore, also a Vidocq Society member. We ate at a little Italian restaurant in South Philly called Gnocchi. Moore is a private investigator and a DNA genealogist with her own company in Virginia called Innovative Forensic Investigations. I told her about the Club House Jane Doe case, and she asked to see the report, so I sent it to her.

BODE labs had reported the top three matches to Club House Jane Doe, with two people in the UK and one in Italy. Coincidentally, the crucifix found with Club House Jane Doe's body had been traced back to a gift shop at the Vatican in Rome, Italy. This went entirely against my theory that she was a local girl from Philadelphia or Lower Bucks County, and I began to think she was from Italy.

Moore used her investigative expertise to build Jane Doe's family tree and traced Club House Jane Doe's great-grandparents to Schuylkill, Pennsylvania. That's a hell of a far shot from the UK and Italy, but Moore was also an investigator, and I trusted her instincts. I asked her to keep digging, and she did. The following Monday morning, Moore sent me screenshots of Jane Doe's family tree, which included the name "Merrybeth Hodgkinson." Moore circled it and said everything pointed to that girl (Merrybeth). She had found the mother's obituary, which read, "Mom was preceded in death by Merrybeth." Yet Moore could not find an obituary for Merrybeth. The Hodgkinson family was from Warminster, Pennsylvania in Bucks County. This surprised me because Warminster is only about 12 miles from Bensalem.

I looked at the family tree and saw she had a brother, Eric Hodgkinson. I looked Eric up and learned that he still lived in Warminster, PA. After finding his phone number, I called and spoke with him. I told him who I was and asked if he had ever had a sibling who vanished. He paused and said, "Yeah, I did... my sister, Merrybeth " He said she went missing in 1992. That fit perfectly because we had estimated she had been dead for two to three years when her body was found. Merrybeth was one of eight siblings and had two children that she had put up for adoption after their birth.

A week before Thanksgiving 2021, with the help of Jen Moore, Club House Jane Doe was finally identified as Merrybeth Hodgkinson. Direct DNA comparisons with one of Merrybeth's siblings matched as a first-degree relative to Club House Jane Doe, and just like Lisa Todd and Jeanette Tambe, Merrybeth had her name back.

I learned that Merrybeth was, in fact, a stripper and had been working at a bar called the Oakford Inn, located by Neshaminy Mall. Coincidentally, the Oakford Inn used to be called the Sandpiper, the same bar Robert Rowan ate at the day Barbara went missing. It was not a go-go bar in 1984. That building was just recently knocked down and is no longer there. However, Merrybeth's family confirmed that she was dancing at the Oakford Inn and living above the bar, in one of the rental rooms, for some time.

I then talked to her other siblings. Merrybeth's oldest sister told me that Merrybeth had a history of mental illness and had been diagnosed as having schizophrenia. Because of that, Merrybeth collected state disability, and her SSI checks were sent to her father's house, although she didn't live there. An old SSI check from October 1992 was salvaged from her father's records. It had never been picked up, collected, or cashed. That told me the approximate time Merrybeth died. That time frame also aligned perfectly with when Montgomery was preying on women—and we already knew he killed one woman in September 1992 and another in March 1993.

The family was not shocked that Merrybeth was dead, but they were taken aback by the fact she had been murdered. And as for the crucifixes found with her remains, none of her siblings seem to know where they came from. It was reported that Merrybeth's mother was a devout Catholic, so that could be the connection.

The criminals who killed Lisa Todd, Merrybeth Hodgkinson, and Jeanette Tambe may not have answered for it yet, but there's no statute of limitations, and the cases are still open. The victims have their names back, and their families have some answers. I can only hope that technology continues to advance and that the investigators who currently have these cases remain stubborn and refuse to give up. I have faith in them.

EPILOGUE

About two months ago, Lily, my cat of fifteen years, passed away. There's an animal shelter at the old Cherokee Day Camp, so I donated her leftover cat food and supplies there. I slowly drove through the old campground and felt sick over how things had changed over the years. Cherokee Day Camp officially closed its doors in 2017. Once a very active and youthful environment, it had transformed into an abandoned, dismal ten acres of neglected land. A long driveway covered by overgrown brush and a remnant of the main building still stood with the name "Cherokee" painted in large letters.

The yellow merry-go-round was the first thing I looked for, but it is no longer there. The pool at the top of the hill was empty and uncovered; windows were boarded up on the buildings. It saddened me to see how much the place that had given me some of my best boyhood memories no longer existed. With time, everything changes; you hope it's for the best, but that's not always the case.

**2019, the abandoned buildings
of Cherokee Day Camp
Credit: Maria Viola Jefferson**

In the past thirty-two years, I have learned that if you want something badly enough and believe in it, you should work for it. I've gotten a few acting jobs in movies and on television, but if I never get an acting job again, it's okay because I did it already. I'm not well-known in the acting world, but I have lived my dream more than once—even if it was just for a few days. In addition, I have appeared on true crime shows. I even got to cry on Paula Zahn's show and work with the Homicide Hunter, Joe Kenda.

As for the cold cases, the naysayers can all go to hell. The work done by Mike Mosiniak, Jennifer Schorn, Jess Bryant, Cathy DeBuono, Yolanda McClary, Jennifer Moore, and me will forever positively impact the families of the victims in this book. They are indeed starfish, and we made a positive difference to them. Many others helped along the way: Dave Nieves; John Monaghan; Fred Harran; and my wife, Heather Hines, who has helped in more ways than I can ever thank her for; my parents, who did a good job raising me; my daughter Caitlin—we grew up together; and Tianna Godsey for her storytelling guidance. I also want to thank my friend and co-author, Maria Viola Jefferson, for helping me write this book and for being patient with me along the way.

Some positive changes from all of this? I am now a member of the Vidocq Society, and I've recently started a non-profit organization named "Cold Case Initiative." We aim to raise money to donate to smaller agencies, providing them the financial support for DNA genealogy on their unsolved Doe and violent crime cases. As I said, cold cases need to be brought up to current standards. Frank Friel and Frank Bender's impact will not be forgotten.

March 7, 2022 was the official day of my retirement from the Bensalem PD. Just about a year earlier than I had initially planned, but necessary, nonetheless. I drove my unmarked police car to headquarters for the last time. I met with Lieutenant Bob Bugsch and turned in my gun, badge, cuffs, and body armor. Bob and I went to high school at Father Judge together, so I'm glad I met with him to return my equipment. A few minutes after I did that, Heather showed up, and I knew she was there by invitation. I walked with Sergeant Adam Kolman to the administration wing of the building, where we were greeted by a large gathering of people, including police employees, civilian employees, Jennifer Schorn from the DA's office, my good friend Erin O'Rourke, and my already retired partner, Dave Nieves.

Erin is a forensic nurse and has helped me with numerous rape and sexual assault cases. She was always helpful when reading toxicology reports on victims, too. Dave and I were a force to be reckoned with when we worked together. We made a great team and closed a lot of cases. He is now a detective with the Chester County District Attorney's Office, and he's making a difference there too.

I then greeted new Director of Public Safety Bill McVey. Just then, my grandkids ran out of his office holding a big, colorful sign that read, "Congrats, Pop, We

Love You." Then my daughter Caitlin and her husband Brian walked out. I almost lost it then, but I managed to keep it together. McVey, Nieves, and Jen Schorn spoke very kindly on my behalf. I couldn't be more thankful to everyone for their support and friendship. When I started working there in 1992, I didn't know anyone. But in the last three decades, that place became my extended home. I didn't make a living there; I made a life there, doing what I loved to do.

The county dispatcher in Doylestown hit the alert tone on the police radio, and it was time for me to sign off as 22-I1 for the last time.

Bucks County to all cars and stations, stand by for a special announcement. On behalf of the Bensalem Township Police Department and Bucks County Department of Emergency Communications, we would like to congratulate Detective Christopher McMullin on his retirement from the Bensalem Police Department after a thirty-year honorable career serving its residents. Your dedication to the department, citizens, and victims will go unrivaled. On this date, 22-I1, badge number 22238, will be signing off the radio with the Bensalem Township Police Department for the last time. We wish you health, happiness, and success in your new position with the Bucks County Sheriff's Office. Stay safe out there, I-1.

I stared at the portable police radio in my hand for a millisecond, which seemed like an eternity. Then I picked it up, keyed up, and took a deep breath, "22-I1 to Bucks; I hope I made a difference; you can take me off the log."

The dispatcher signed me off, and just like that, I retired. As I hugged my friends and family, I felt a sense of peace that I'd never experienced before. I thought of Nan and Frank Friel.

It seemed like just a month ago, I was a twenty-two-year-old kid getting sworn in by Judge Brown with Frank Friel looking on. Now, I'm fifty-two and have reached the finish line. I should be happy… and I am. It's bittersweet since I will no longer work there, doing what I love. After all, I was at the Bensalem PD for over half my life, and now that chapter is finally closing. And although I have officially signed off as 22-I1 for the last time, I'm not done yet. Fred Harran, my friend for thirty years since day one at the Bensalem PD, retired as the director of public safety on December 30, 2021. Harran was the sheriff-elect of Bucks County and retired from the Bensalem Police Department to take that office. He was sworn in on January 3, 2022. When the opportunity presented itself to take on a new position with him, I accepted it. On March 28, 2022, I was sworn in as a lieutenant deputy sheriff and signed back on the radio as 85-L1, once again working alongside Harran.

My favorite movie of all time is *A Bronx Tale*, and to borrow and slightly alter a quote from one of the greatest living storytellers of all time, Chazz Palminteri, "This is just another cop tale." Now, if I could just get Foreigner inducted into the Rock and Roll Hall of Fame.